## I. Introduction

Numerous studies have documented the sizable gains to consumers that followed federal deregulation of various transportation sectors.[1] Each of these studies estimated the effects of federal deregulation on price by comparing post-deregulation prices with estimates of what prices would have been had economic regulation continued.[2] While indisputably informative, such analyses nonetheless assume that regulation is an all-or-nothing phenomenon; it either exists or it does not. In fact, transportation regulations take a variety of forms including rate regulation, entry restrictions, and the provision of antitrust immunity for decisions made jointly by competitors. To date, no study has attempted to estimate the independent effect on transportation prices from these different types of economic regulations.

This study fills that gap by estimating the relationship between trucking rates and three different types of state-level regulations: (1) the strictness with which rates are regulated; (2) the requirements placed on motor carriers seeking to enter the market; and (3) whether the state provides antitrust immunity for decisions made by motor carrier rate

---

[1] With respect to airline deregulation, a 1990 Department of Transportation study concluded that "air travelers have benefited from the changes brought about under deregulation by receiving more service at a lower cost." (U. S. Department of Transportation (1990), Executive Summary, p. 1.) For railroads, which were deregulated by the 1980 Staggers Act, a 1990 GAO Study concluded that "shippers have benefited from reduced railroad regulation. Since 1980, rail rates, adjusted for inflation, have declined an average of about 22 percent. In addition, service has improved: train reliability has increased and freight car shortages have declined." (U.S. General Accounting Office (1990), p. 4. See also Barnekov and Kleit (1990) and Burton (1993)). Winston *et al.* (1990) examined both railroads and interstate trucking, the latter having been deregulated by the 1980 Motor Carrier Act (MCA) and concluded that federal deregulation of these two industries provides net benefits to consumers of over $16 billion (1988 dollars) each and every year.

[2] The focus of this study is economic regulation, *e.g.*, rate regulation and entry controls. We do not examine safety regulation. Unless otherwise noted, we will use the word "regulation" to refer only to economic, and not safety, regulation. For a discussion of safety regulation, see Alexander (1992).

1

bureaus. By combining a cross-section of intrastate trucking rates from these states with information on the motor carrier laws and regulations in place at the time, we can estimate the relationships between particular types of regulations and trucking rates.

Our basic conclusions are consistent with previous studies which found that motor carrier regulations tend to raise rates. In the less-than-truckload ("LTL") sector (shipments of less than 10,000 pounds), there is a positive relationship between each of the three regulations studied and intrastate trucking rates. That is, motor carrier freight rates tend to be significantly higher in states that strictly regulate rates, in states that impose significant restrictions on new entrants, and in states that provide antitrust immunity for rate bureau decisions. Entry restrictions have the largest rate-increasing effect: in the LTL sector, significant entry restrictions raise trucking rates over 20 percent. With regard to the other two types of regulations analyzed, strict rate regulation raises LTL trucking rates over 5 percent, and antitrust immunity raises LTL trucking rates over 12 percent.

In the truckload ("TL") sector (shipments of more than 10,000 pounds), the results are somewhat different. A strong positive relationship emerges between trucking rates and the degree to which the state regulates those rates. This positive relationship is stronger than that found in the LTL sector. Specifically, states that regulate rates strictly have TL rates over 32 percent higher than states that do not regulate rates strictly. Unlike the results for the LTL sector, however, there is no significant relationship between TL trucking rates and either entry requirements or the provision of antitrust immunity.

## II. The Regulation of Motor Carriers

Motor freight transportation would appear to approximate the textbook definition for atomistic competition: modest (or nonexistent) economies of scale and ease of entry into and exit from particular routes. (Wilson and Dooley (1993))[3] Yet, despite these characteristics, the trucking industry was highly regulated at the federal level from 1935 to 1980 and in most states for even longer. Regulations typically took the form of entry restrictions (*e.g.*, carriers were provided authority to transport a particular commodity on a particular route only after showing that such service met a compelling public need) and rate regulations (*e.g.*, tariffs were approved by the relevant regulatory agency and could only be changed up or down after a demonstration that the proposed changes were justified.)

At the national level, these regulations were the focus of considerable economic and political debate in the 1970s, culminating in the passage of the Motor Carrier Act ("MCA") in 1980. The MCA, in conjunction with its liberal interpretation by the Interstate Commerce Commission ("ICC"), eliminated large parts of the federal regulatory regime. In particular, motor carriers could enter interstate markets much more easily and interstate motor carriers could change their prices with significantly less regulatory oversight. As noted above, economic studies have shown that these changes yielded significant benefits for consumers.

---

[3] Keeler (1989) used the survivorship technique to obtain results consistent with the view that trucking firms experience modest economies of scale. Yet, Keeler stated that using this finding to support reregulation of the trucking industry would be "seriously wrong for several reasons." He then elaborated by citing to (1) the mobility of trucks, which implies that trucking markets would in many instances be national in scope; (2) the generally low level of sunk costs in the trucking industry; and (3) empirical studies documenting the gains to consumers and shippers from trucking deregulation.

At the federal level, an important remaining vestige of the pre-MCA regulatory regime is the provision of limited antitrust immunity for rate bureaus.[4] The effect on rates from providing immunity to rate bureaus is not clear. On the one hand, as the Department of Justice has argued before the ICC, immunity from the antitrust laws could raise rates by facilitating tacit or explicit collusion among the rate bureau members.[5] Supporters of antitrust immunity for rate bureaus (Hausman (1983) and Tye (1987)) counter by arguing that immunity is necessary to foster the efficient exchange of information among the bureaus' members. Under the assumption that the industry is competitive, any benefits stemming from the efficient exchange of information would be passed on to shippers as lower rates.

At the state level, the extent of motor carrier regulation varies significantly. Some states have completely deregulated the motor carrier industry. Other states strictly limit entry by providing operating certificates to prospective entrants only after a showing that the entry fills a compelling public need that cannot be met by existing carriers. Some states continue to regulate rates strictly; others provide for little or no regulatory review of rate changes. While every state permits motor carriers to belong to rate bureaus, only about half of them grant motor carriers antitrust immunity for the bureaus' joint activities, such as rate making and scheduling.

---

[4] The MCA grants antitrust immunity for some but not all of a rate bureau's activities. Rate bureaus cannot, for example, collectively establish single-line rates, that is, rates on routes that can be handled by a single carrier. By contrast, the MCA does provide antitrust immunity for joint-line rates (routes involving more than one carrier) and for general rate increases (across the board increases on an entire menu of rates.)

[5] Petition of the United States Department of Justice for an Order Requiring the Members of the Rocky Mountain Motor Tariff Bureau to Show Cause Why Their Antitrust Immunity to Discuss and Agree on General Rate Increases Should Not Be Withdrawn, filed with the Interstate Commerce Commission, December 19, 1989.

4

Decisions regarding the regulation of the motor carrier industry continue to arise at both the federal and state level. Notwithstanding the significant reforms contained in the 1980 MCA, economic regulations, such as tariff-filing requirements and continued antitrust immunity for some rate bureau decisions, remain at the federal level. In addition, forty-two states continue to regulate intrastate truckers, and states frequently consider proposals to relax or to expand the extent to which truckers are regulated in their states.[6] Such regulation has an important economic impact because approximately two-thirds of all shipments are intrastate. (Allen *et al.* (1990), p. 9) Proponents of continued or expanded economic motor carrier regulation typically claim that certain regulations provide stability to the industry, prevent "destructive competition", and do not contribute to higher prices. Our empirical analysis provides a direct test of this last claim.

## III. Data

### A. Rate Data

Our data contain point-to-point trucking rates, both interstate and intrastate, announced by motor carrier rate bureaus and on file with the relevant regulatory agencies in the continental U.S. during the spring of 1987. Each intrastate route has a companion interstate route emanating for the same origin city and terminating in a city of similar size

---

[6] See, for instance, the discussion of state laws and regulatory initiatives in *Consumer Cost of Continued State Motor Carrier Regulation*, Twenty-first Report by the Committee of Government Operations, House Report 101-813 (October 5, 1990). In 1992, the Michigan Public Service Commission reconsidered its state's trucking regulations. See, *In the Matter of the Proposed Revisions to the Motor Carrier Rules, Order Publishing Proposed Revisions to the Motor Carrier Rules and Providing Notice of Hearing*, Case No. T-1210, Michigan Public Service Commission (released August 14, 1992).

after travelling roughly the same distance. The data contain 708 of these "triads" with origins in thirty-nine states.[7]

For each route the data contain the rates, denominated in cents per hundred pounds shipped, for a variety of commodity classes (typically twelve) and for a number of weight categories (typically less than 500 pounds through 20000 pounds), as well as the mileage between the origin and destination cities.

Three points about the rate data deserve mention. First, the rates are those filed with a regulatory agency by a motor carrier rate bureau.[8] While filed rates are available to shippers, they often are not the rates actually charged. Nonetheless, we believe that the filed rates should be representative of those actually charged, especially when discounting is accounted for (see below).[9]

Second, carriers typically offer shippers discounts from filed rates. We account for discounting by reducing the filed rate by the discount generally available. We discount all interstate rates by 27.81 percent, which is the average of the discounts provided by rate

---

[7] The eleven excluded states fall into three categories. First, the rate data do not contain intrastate rates for the eight states that had deregulated their motor carrier industries by 1987: Alaska, Arizona, Delaware, Florida, Maine, New Jersey, Vermont, and Wisconsin. Second, Hawaii was excluded because interstate trucking rates cannot exist there. Third, Montana and Wyoming were excluded because the dataset did not contain any intrastate rate information for these states.

[8] At the interstate level, the rates were filed by one of the ten dominant interstate rate bureaus, whose operating areas (generally) do not overlap. At the intrastate level, various motor carrier rate bureaus typically operate; the data contain the rates filed by one of the larger (or the largest) rate bureaus operating in the state.

[9] We note that there appears no way other than relying on filed rates to obtain data on intrastate rates from enough states to conduct an analysis as comprehensive as this. Actual transaction prices are not publicly available, and data on particular carriers (such as those contained in the American Trucking Association's Annual Report) are not state-specific. (See, *e.g.*, Ying and Keeler (1991) and Winston *et al.* (1990)).

bureaus during the spring of 1987.[10]  For intrastate rates, we use the discounts typically

offered during this period as reported in Allen *et al.* (1990).[11]

Third, the rates analyzed in this study are <u>class</u> rates.  Motor carriers typically offer

two types of common carrier rates:  class rates and commodity rates.  Commodity rates, as

the name implies, pertain to a particular commodity (such as lumber) and are typically offered

to larger-volume shippers who can provide truckload quantities.  Class rates, by contrast, are

offers to ship goods in particular classes at specified rates.  Each product is assigned to a

numbered class, and rates are higher for higher-numbered classes.  An alternative to common

carrier shipments is contract carriage, which occurs when relatively large shippers contract

directly with carriers for a series of shipments of merchandise over a period of time.  Such

shipments are moved under "contract" rates, but information from these contracts is not

publicly available.

Recent data do not exist on the proportion of shipments handled under class -- as

opposed to commodity or contract -- rates.  Detailed data on interstate common carriage

shipments were collected by the ICC in the late 1970s and early 1980s.  According to the

Motor Carrier Ratemaking Study Commission ("MCRSC") (1983, p. 182) approximately

87.9% of common carriage interstate shipments in 1980 were made under class rates, 5.1%

---

[10] We obtained information on interstate discounts from the ICC.  The applicable
discounts were culled by ICC staff from filings made by the interstate rate bureaus.  Because
the variation around the average was relatively small, and because it is difficult to determine
which discount to apply to routes that traverse the territory of two rate bureaus, we chose to
use the simple average for all interstate rates.

[11] Of the thirty-nine states included in this study, thirteen do not permit discounting.  For
those states that do permit discounting, Allen *et al.* (1990) attempted to obtain two estimates
for the discount typically available -- one from a shipper, and another from a state regulatory
official.  For states in which they obtained two estimates for the typical discount, we
conducted our analysis using the higher discount, the lower discount, and the average of the
two.  Our empirical results do not change depending on which of these intrastate discounts are
used; the results reported below use the higher discount (where more than one was available).

under commodity rates, 1.9% under "commodity column" rates, and 2.6% under exception rates. Thus, in 1980 the overwhelming percentage of common carrier shipments were moved under class rates.[12] The percentage of common carrier shipments handled under class rates was high for less-than-truckload (LTL) shipments (90.0%) but significantly lower for truckload (TL) shipments (27.1%). These figures imply that our data may reflect more accurately the rate structure for LTL shipments than for TL ones.

As noted above, the data contain rates for a number of different classes for each route. After examining the data, we discovered that the rates for various classes, holding route and weight fixed, were very highly correlated. In many cases, the rates were perfectly correlated, that is, the rate for class 100 was exactly twice that for class 50, and the rate for class 150 exactly three times that for class 50. Given the high correlation across classes, we arbitrarily chose to analyze class 100 rates.

We focus on three different weights: less-than-500 pounds, 2000 pounds, and 20000 pounds. The first two are less-than-truckload (LTL) categories; the last is a truckload (TL) weight. We have two reasons for focusing on these weight levels. First, our empirical analysis (described below) uses rate data from both interstate and intrastate routes. These three weights had the largest number of "matches" in the data. Second, it has been argued that any benefits of antitrust immunity and collective decision making are more likely to arise in the LTL, rather than the TL, sector of the industry, where some sunk costs arise and coordination among carriers could conceivably help carriers avert "destructive competition." We thus will test for such benefits in both sectors.

---

[12] The data indicated that shipments under class rates tended to be shorter in distance and smaller in size than those under commodity rates. Of the total amount of interstate traffic carried under common carrier rates, shipments under class rates accounted for approximately 73% of the revenues collected and 49% of the tonnage shipped.

B. Summary Statistics

The data contain routes, both intrastate and interstate, with origins in thirty-nine states. We have added to the rate and mileage figures the populations of the origin and destination cities, taken from the 1980 Census. Table 1 contains some basic summary statistics for the routes for each of the three weight categories included in the analysis.[13]

---

[13] In order for a triad to be included, the computerized rate base had to have an interstate rate and an intrastate rate for the weight class of interest.

**Table 1**
**SUMMARY STATISTICS**
(various weight categories)

| | WEIGHT CATEGORY | | |
| --- | --- | --- | --- |
| | < 500 lbs. | 2000 lbs. | 20000 lbs. |
| Number of routes | 673 | 644 | 290 |
| Number of states with origin cities | 38 | 36 | 17 |
| Average mileage (std. deviation) | | | |
| intrastate route | 198 (115) | 200 (117) | 237 (125) |
| interstate route | 202 (113) | 204 (114) | 242 (123) |
| Average population (std. deviation) | | | |
| origin city | 214,015 (601,663) | 197,291 (546,637) | 307,730 (842,485) |
| destination, intrastate | 67,119 (156,450) | 57,110 (89,113) | 85,819 (218,027) |
| destination, interstate | 62,290 (111,889) | 59,076 (104,289) | 70,928 (129,116) |

Table 1 reveals that the intrastate and interstate routes are, on average, approximately the same length and terminate in cities of approximately the same size. Origin cities are, on average, approximately three to four times larger than destination cities. Figures M1-M3 are maps showing, for each weight class, the states included in the analysis.

10

# FIGURE M1

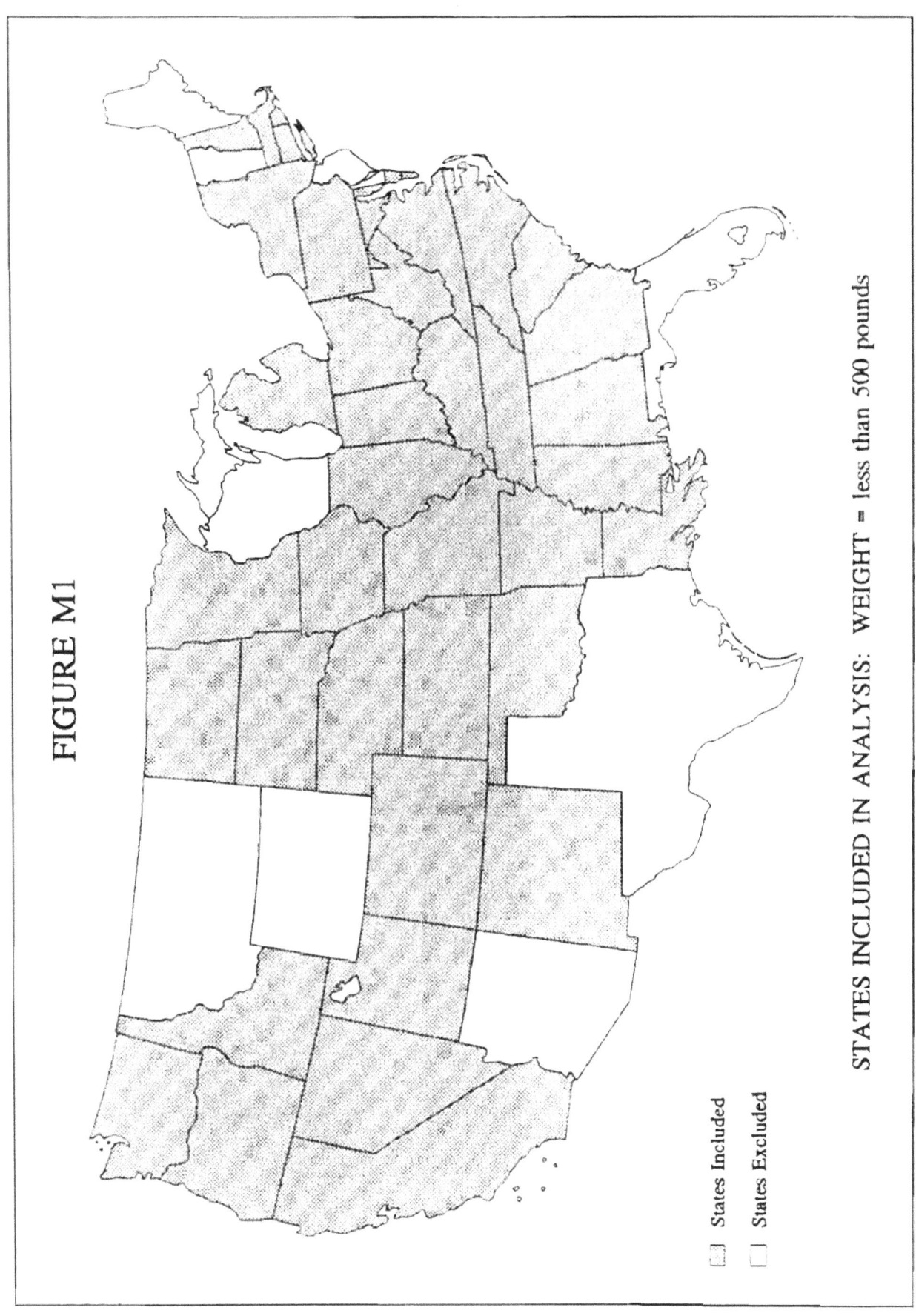

STATES INCLUDED IN ANALYSIS:  WEIGHT = less than 500 pounds

□ States Included

□ States Excluded

# FIGURE M2

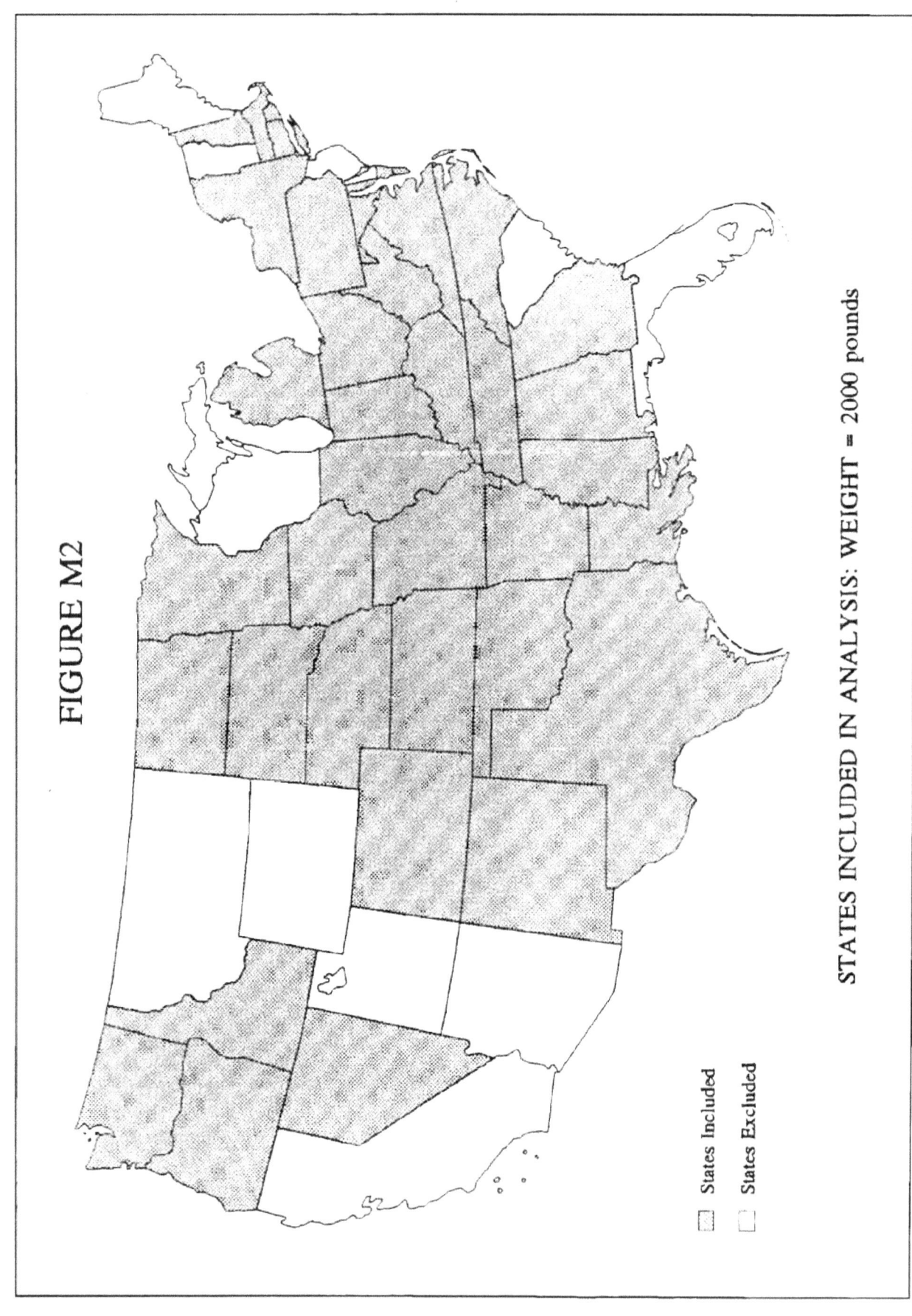

STATES INCLUDED IN ANALYSIS: WEIGHT = 2000 pounds

☒ States Included

☐ States Excluded

# FIGURE M3

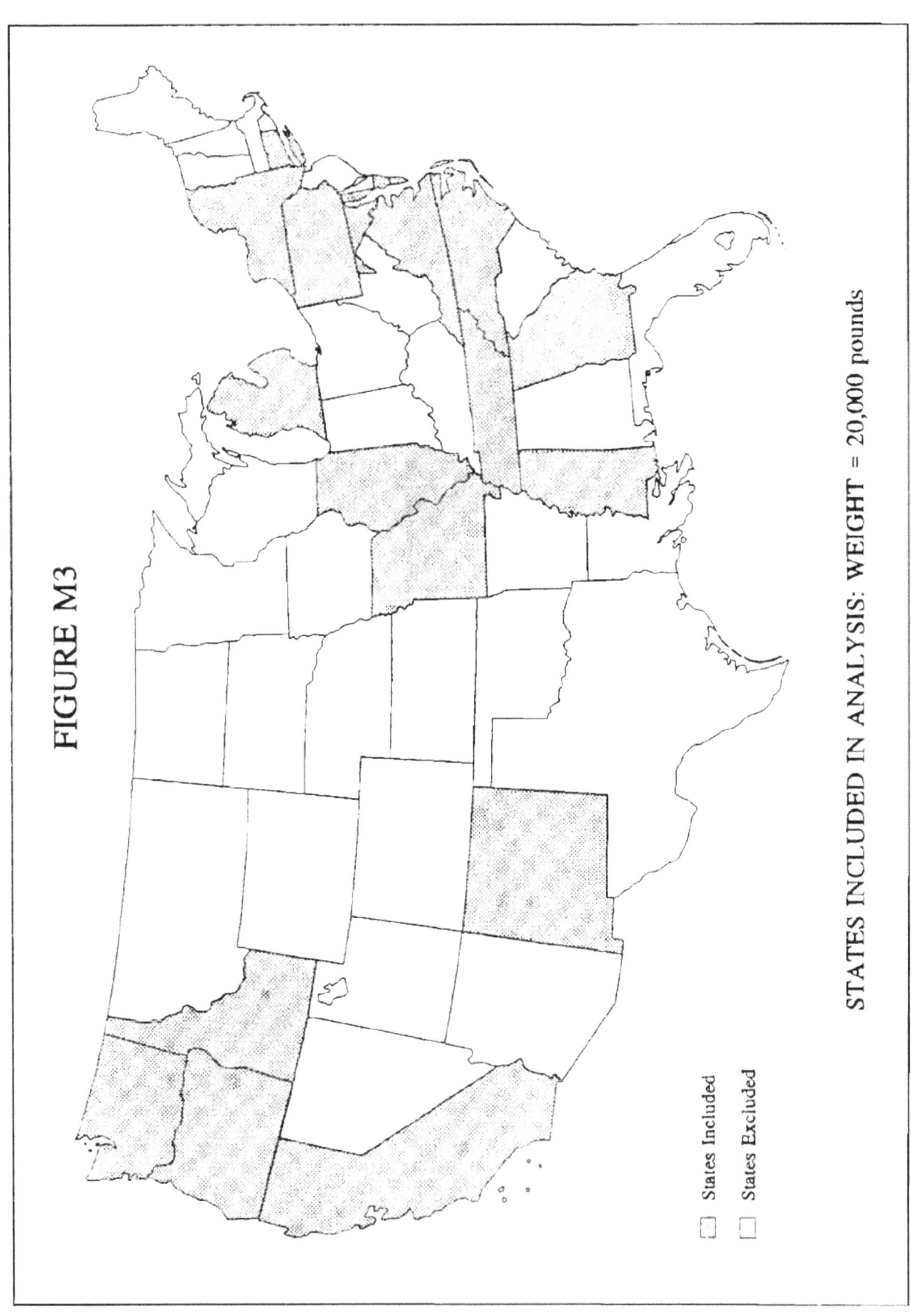

STATES INCLUDED IN ANALYSIS: WEIGHT = 20,000 pounds

☐ States Included
☐ States Excluded

## C. State-level regulations

Our information on the motor carrier regulations in place in the various states in 1987 is taken from a survey of state motor carrier regulations compiled by Daniel Baker, an attorney affiliated with the Transportation Lawyers' Association (TLA). On behalf of the TLA, Baker annually surveys individuals familiar with the motor carrier laws and regulations that exist in each state.

The Baker survey contains a number of questions concerning motor carrier regulation. We use the answers to the following four questions to characterize a state's regulatory regime. In brackets following the questions are the possible responses.[14]

(1)     To what extent does the state regulate motor common carrier rates? **[strict regulation; not strict regulation]**

(2)     What is required to obtain motor common carrier authority from the state? **[strict requirements; not strict requirements]**

(3)     How effective are protests to motor common carrier applications? **[very effective; somewhat effective; not effective]**

(4)     Does antitrust immunity exist for tariff bureaus that publish motor carrier rates? **[YES, bureaus are immune; NO, bureaus are not immune]**

Question 1 is a measure of the degree to which state regulators are involved in establishing and maintaining a particular tariff structure. Note that protests by incumbent carriers (question (3)) can only be effective in states where significant entry barriers already exist (question (2)). Finally, question (4) pertains to whether rate bureau actions are shielded from antitrust scrutiny at the state level.

---

[14] In the actual survey, respondents were offered more choices than are contained in the brackets. The responses in the brackets distill the responses into two categories for use in the empirical analysis. A copy of the 1987 Baker survey is contained in Appendix A of this report.

Based on the responses to these questions, we characterize state-level trucking regulation with four 0-1 dummy variables.

RATEREG = dummy variable equal to one if the state strictly regulates motor carrier rates; zero otherwise.

ENTRY1 = dummy variable equal to one if the state has strict entry requirements and if protests by incumbent carriers against applications for new entry are very effective; zero otherwise.

ENTRY2 = dummy variable equal to one if the state has strict entry requirements and if protests by incumbent carriers against applications for new entry are somewhat effective; zero otherwise.

IMMUNE = dummy variable equal to one if the state grants rate bureaus antitrust immunity; zero otherwise.

Table 2 contains the number of states in which these four variables assumes the value one for each of the three weight classes analyzed.

**Table 2**

**Number of states with various motor carrier regulations in 1987**
**(percent of total in parentheses)**

WEIGHT CATEGORY
(n = number of states included in analysis)

|  | < 500 lbs. (n=38) | 2000 lbs. (n=36) | 20000 lbs. (n=17) |
|---|---|---|---|
| Variable |  |  |  |
| RATEREG | 19 (50%) | 18 (50%) | 11 (65%) |
| ENTRY1 | 8 (21%) | 9 (25%) | 4 (24%) |
| ENTRY2 | 23 (61%) | 23 (64%) | 9 (53%) |
| IMMUNE | 22 (58%) | 21 (58%) | 12 (71%) |

Figures M4-M6 are maps showing the status of each regulation (rate regulation, entry restrictions, and antitrust immunity) in each state in the continental U.S. in the spring of 1987.

# RATE REGULATION BY STATE, 1987

States that have strict rate regulation:

AL, CA, GA, IL, LA, MI, MS, MO, NE, NV,

NM, NC, OK, OR, PA, RI, SC, TX, WA, WV

States that do not have strict rate regulation:

AR, CO, CT, ID, IN, IA, KS, KY, MD, MA,

MN, NH, NY, ND, OH, SD, TN, UT, VA

States not included in analysis:

AZ, DE, FL, ME, MT, NJ, VT, WI, WY

# FIGURE M4

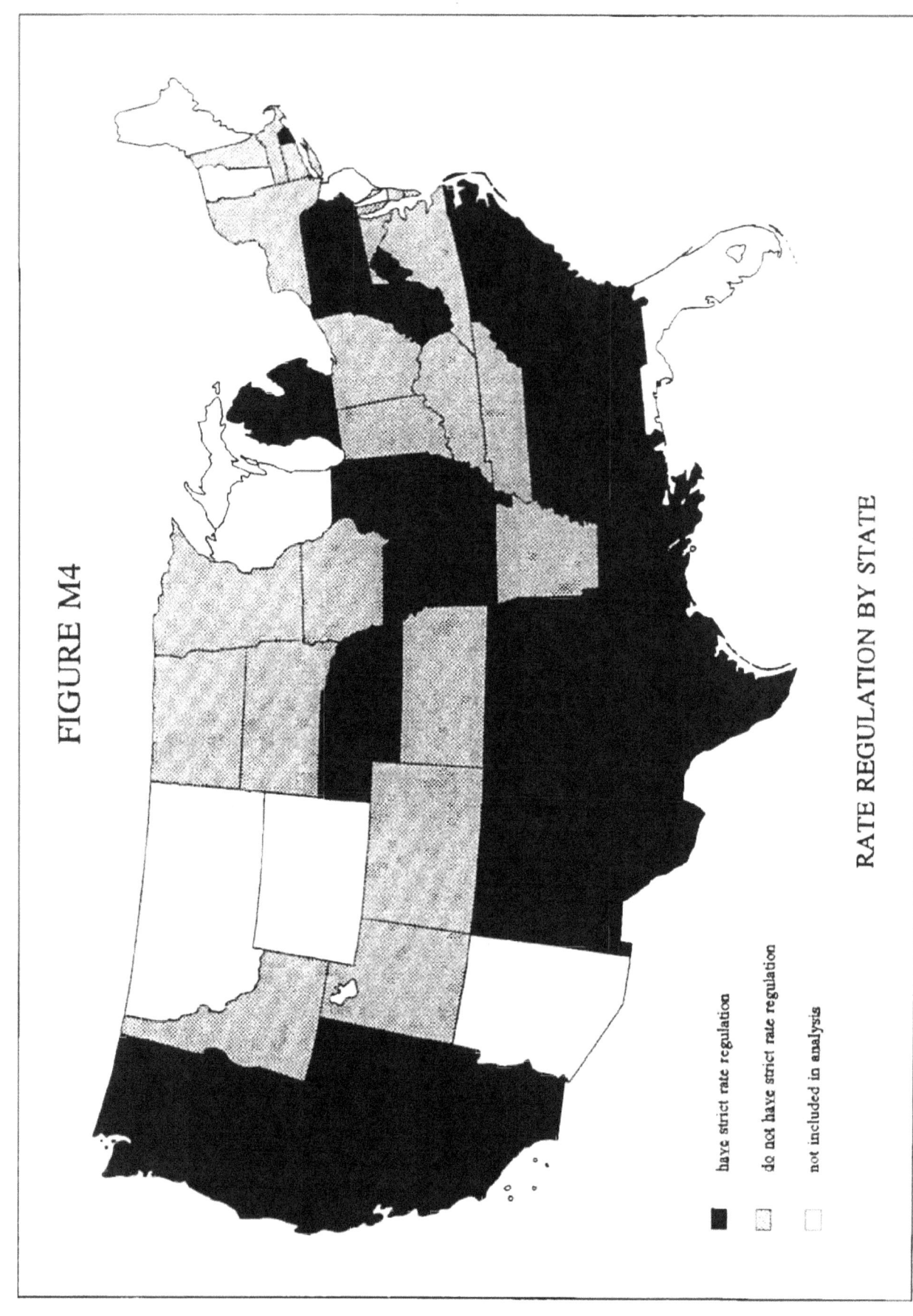

RATE REGULATION BY STATE

■   have strict rate regulation

☐   do not have strict rate regulation

☐   not included in analysis

# ENTRY REGULATION BY STATE, 1987

States that impose very strict entry requirements:

AL, LA, NC, OH, OK, OR, TN, TX, WA

States that impose somewhat strict entry requirements:

AR, CO, CT, GA, IL, IN, IA, KY, MA, MI,

MN, MS, MO, NE, NV, NH, NM, ND, PA, RI,

SD, VA, WV

States with relatively low entry requirements:

CA, ID, KS, MD, NY, SC, UT

States not included in analysis:

AZ, DE, FL, ME, MT, NJ, VT, WI, WY

# FIGURE M5

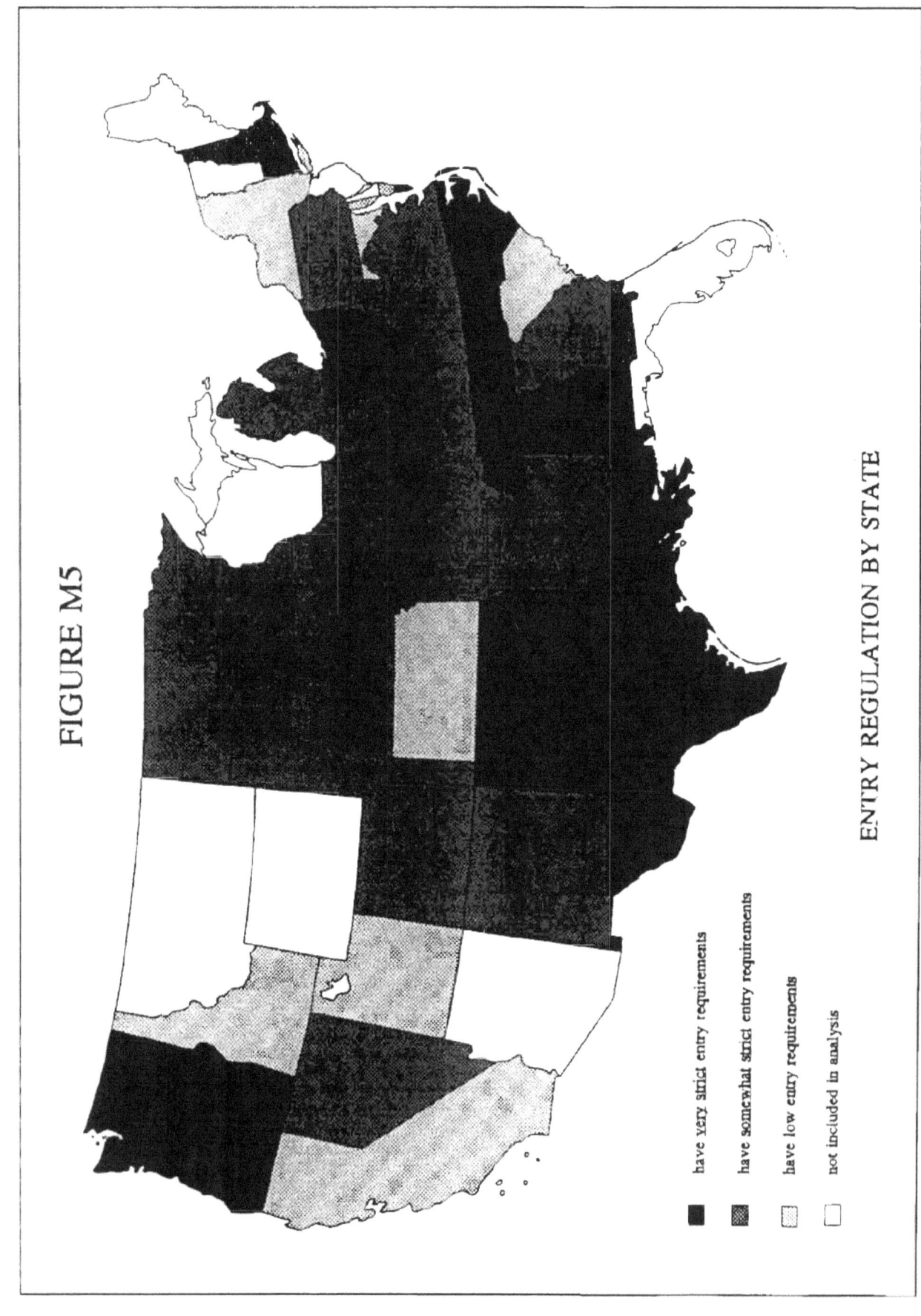

■ have very strict entry requirements

▨ have somewhat strict entry requirements

▢ have low entry requirements

☐ not included in analysis

ENTRY REGULATION BY STATE

# ANTITRUST IMMUNITY BY STATE, 1987

States that provide antitrust immunity to motor carriers:

CA, GA, ID, IL, KS, KY, MA, MI, MN, MO,

NE, NV, NM, NY, NC, OK, OR, PA, RI, SC,

TX, VA, WV

States that do not provide antitrust immunity:

AL, AR, CO, CT, IN, IA, LA, MD, MS, NH,

ND, OH, SD, TN, UT, WA

States not included in analysis:

AZ, DE, FL, ME, MT, NJ, VT, WI, WY

# FIGURE M6

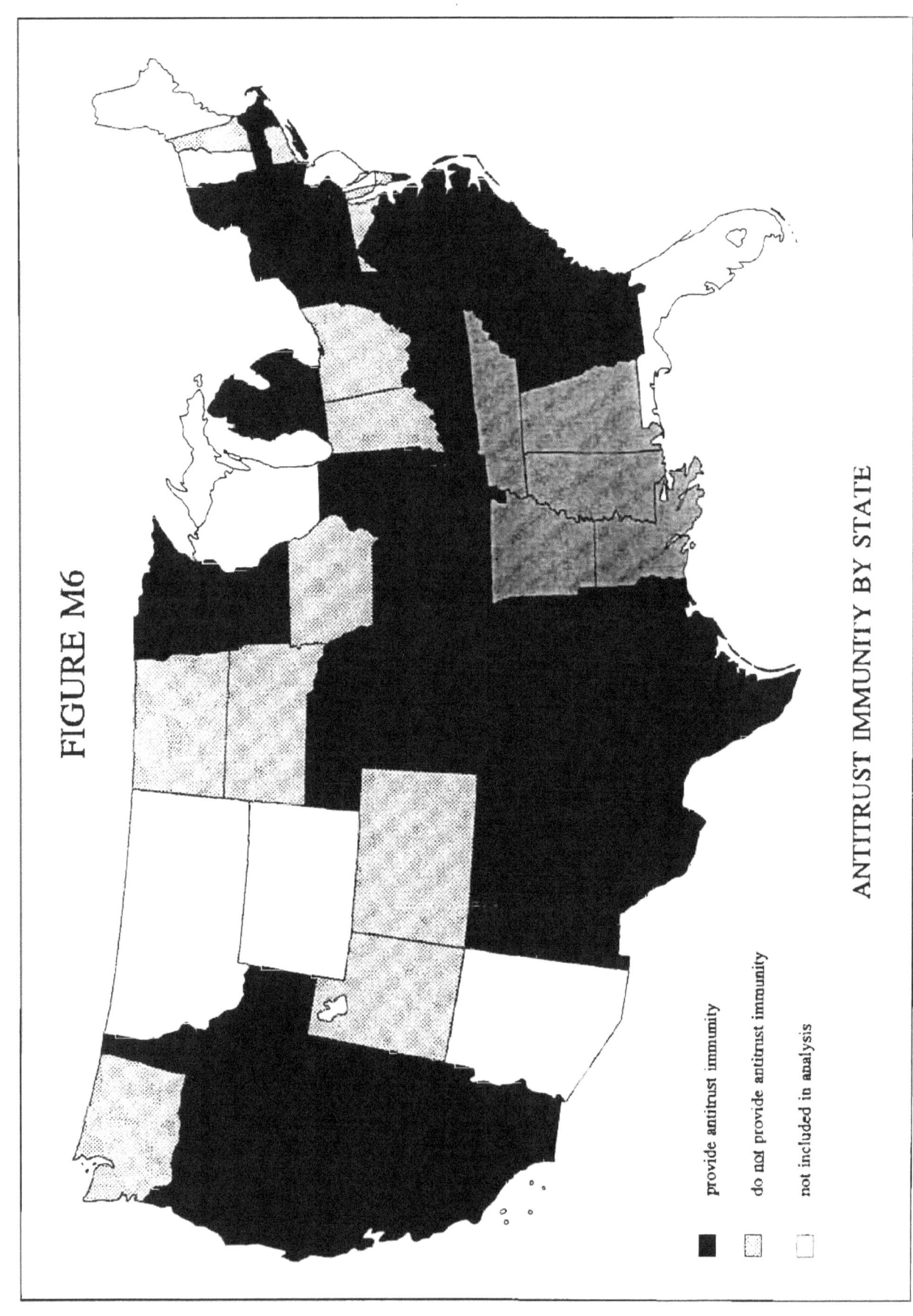

ANTITRUST IMMUNITY BY STATE

provide antitrust immunity

do not provide antitrust immunity

not included in analysis

22

Our aim is to estimate the independent effect on intrastate trucking rates from each of these four regulatory variables. In other words, we seek to estimate how trucking rates change when a particular regulation changes, holding constant the status of the other regulations included in the analysis. In reviewing our regulation variables, we discovered that some regulations tended to occur together. That is, states with one regulation (say, strict rate regulation) tended also to have another regulation (say, strict entry controls.) This empirical fact requires that we interpret our results carefully. Suppose, for example, that we wish to estimate the relationship between regulation A and trucking rates, but it turns out that regulation A only exists in states that also impose regulation B. In such circumstances, the coefficient on regulation A provides an estimate of the likely effect on trucking rates from imposing regulation A *provided that* regulation B already exists. In this example, we cannot obtain an estimate of the likely effect on trucking rates from imposing regulation A in states where regulation B does not exist currently. We conclude this section, therefore, with a brief discussion of the degree to which these state regulatory variables tend to occur together and how this influences the interpretation of the empirical results.

Most states with strict rate regulation also have strict entry requirements. Specifically, in the less than 500 pound analysis, of the 19 states with strict rate regulation fully 17 also have somewhat or very strict entry requirements. In the 2000 pound analysis, *every* state with strict rate regulation also has somewhat or very strict entry requirements. In the 20000 pound analysis, of the 11 states with strict rate regulation 10 also have somewhat or very strict entry requirements. This pattern indicates that the coefficient on the variable RATEREG should be interpreted for the most part (in the case of the 2000 pound analysis, in its entirety) as estimating the relationship between strict rate regulation and trucking rates *provided that* somewhat or very strict entry requirements already exist.[15]

The other regulatory variables are not as highly correlated, and we conclude that the variation is sufficient that we need not qualify the empirical results in the manner described in the previous paragraph. With respect to strict rate regulation (RATEREG) and antitrust immunity (IMMUNE), there is some tendency for states to have both regulations but there also is some variation. Specifically, in both the less than 500 pound and the 2000 pound analyses, four states have RATEREG=1 and IMMUNE=0 and seven states have the opposite. In the 20000 pound analysis the comparable numbers are two states and three states.

Finally, while states that provide antitrust immunity for rate bureaus do tend also to impose strict entry requirements, there appears to be enough variation to identify the relationships between these regulations and trucking rates. In the less than 500 pound analysis, of the 22 states with antitrust immunity, five had low entry requirements. Comparable amounts of variation exist in the 2000 (20000) pound analyses; of the 21 (12) states with antitrust immunity, 3 (3) have low entry requirements.

## IV. Empirical Estimation of the Effects of Regulation

### A. Hypotheses

As discussed in the previous section, we examine three types of state-level motor carrier regulations: rate setting regulations; entry regulations; and regulations providing

---

[15] We note, however, that we do not have to qualify similarly the estimated relationship between trucking rates and entry controls because a number of states that impose entry requirements (either somewhat or very strict) do not also impose strict rate regulation.

antitrust immunity for the joint decisions made by intrastate rate bureaus. Based on economic theory and past research, we have a number of hypotheses concerning the relationships between these regulatory variables and trucking rates.

### 1. Direct Hypotheses

We expect a positive relationship between trucking rates and the extent to which state regulators are involved in establishing and maintaining a particular tariff structure. In principle, active rate regulation by a state could contribute to lower trucking rates. This could arise *if* the trucking industry possessed characteristics conducive to noncompetitive pricing, *e.g.*, significant economies of scale and significant sunk costs. The general academic consensus on this issue, however, is that this is not the case. (See, for example, Keeler (1989).) We therefore hypothesize that rates will be higher in states that actively regulate trucking rates.

We also predict a positive relationship between trucking rates and the severity of entry regulations. At the federal level, the passage of the MCA in 1980 and subsequent interpretations by the Interstate Commerce Commission made entry into new routes by existing carriers and by new carriers much easier, leading to significantly lower trucking rates. (Winston *et al.* (1990) and Ying and Keeler (1991).) Moreover, given experiences at the federal level, we expect this relationship to be especially strong in states where incumbent carriers can effectively deter or delay new entry by protesting prospective entrants' applications for operating authority. (U.S. Department of Transportation (1979), pp. 5-6)

Finally, as mentioned earlier, it is not possible to predict the relationship between trucking rates and the provision of antitrust immunity for rate bureaus. On the one hand, immunity from the antitrust laws could raise rates by facilitating coordination among the rate bureau members. On the other hand, immunity might be necessary to foster the efficient

25

exchange of information among the bureaus' members, and to promote the efficient use of existing capacity.

## 2. Interactive Hypotheses

We also examine somewhat more complex hypotheses to allow for interactions among the three types of regulations. First, even if on average there is a positive relationship between trucking rates and antitrust immunity for rate bureaus, it could be diminished, perhaps eliminated, in states where entry is largely unobstructed. The argument here is straightforward: attempts by rate bureaus to raise rates behind the shield of antitrust immunity would attract entry (absent regulatory barriers), thereby defeating the attempted rate increase. Consequently, we hypothesize that the relationship between trucking rates and antitrust immunity will be stronger (weaker) in states with strict (low) entry requirements. Similarly, we hypothesize that the relationship between trucking rates and entry restrictions will be stronger (weaker) in states that grant (do not grant) antitrust immunity to rate bureaus. We test these hypotheses by analyzing only those observations from states with strict entry requirements (or from states that grant antitrust immunity). We expect the *combination* of antitrust immunity and strict entry requirements to contribute to significantly higher trucking rates.[16]

Second, we consider whether the relationship between antitrust immunity and trucking rates is different in states with strict rate regulation than in those without strict rate regulation. We hypothesize that the combination of antitrust immunity and strict rate regulation could

---

[16] One might hypothesize further that the positive effect on rates from combining strict entry requirements and antitrust immunity would be weaker in states with strict rate regulation. This might arise because strict rate regulation already exerts a positive effect on rates, thereby limiting the additional impact from including strict entry requirements and antitrust immunity. Testing for this effect would require segmenting the data even further. We are prohibited from doing so, however, because of the degree of collinearity among our regulatory variables.

facilitate collusion among the motor carriers operating in a state. Incentives to reduce rates could be dampened considerably in states where truckers can legally meet to discuss rates and other matters, and where rates cannot be reduced without regulatory approval. Under this hypothesis, the relationship between antitrust immunity and trucking rates would be stronger in states that also strictly regulated trucking rates.

Finally, we consider whether the relationship between entry regulations and trucking rates is different in states that regulate rates strictly. Two competing hypotheses exist here. First, it might be the case that states with both strict rate regulation and strict entry controls (as opposed to one or the other) are ones in which the state legislature and regulators are particularly sensitive to incumbent truckers' concerns that deregulation of rates and entry would diminish their ability to serve shippers profitably. If this view of regulation holds, the combination of these two regulations would facilitate collusion among the incumbent carriers and lead to higher trucking rates. Under this view, we would expect the positive relationship between entry restrictions and trucking rates to be even stronger in states that also regulate rates strictly. On the other hand, free entry might not reduce rates in states with strict rate regulation. Instead, it could be the case that firms enter until industry profits are zero, resulting in an inefficient use of capacity as any supra-competitive profits are competed away on other margins.[17] Under this alternative line of reasoning, the positive relationship between trucking rates and strict rate regulation would not be stronger in states that also strictly regulate entry. Similarly, this view would imply that the positive relationship between entry restrictions and rates would not be stronger in states that also regulate rates strictly.

---

[17] Douglas and Miller (1974) discuss this effect in the context of the regulated airline industry.

### B. Estimation Approach

Estimating the relationship between state motor carrier regulations and intrastate trucking rates is conceptually straightforward: regress intrastate rates from a number of states (the dependent variable) on a series of regulatory variables and other variables likely to affect trucking rates (collectively, the independent variables). Prior to combining into one analysis the rate and regulation variables from a number of states, we reviewed carefully the pattern of rates on file in each of the states. This review indicated that <u>within</u> a particular state for a particular weight category there is a strong statistical relationship between the filed rate and the distance of the route. In other words, the rates for a particular weight category <u>within</u> a particular state can be largely explained by the following simple formula:

**(1)** $$R_{ijk} = \alpha_{jk} + \beta_{jk} * M_{ijk} + u_{ijk}$$

where,

| | | |
|---|---|---|
| $R_{ijk}$ | = | the log of the rate for route i, weight j, state k |
| $M_{ijk}$ | = | the log of mileage for route i, weight j, state k |
| $u_{ijk}$ | = | error term with mean 0 and variance $\sigma^2$ |
| $\alpha_{jk}, \beta_{jk}$ | = | state-specific parameters subject to estimation for weight j and state k. |

We ran equation (1) separately for each of the states and each of the weights included in our dataset. This involved 88 separate regressions: 37 for the less than 500 pound category, 35 for the 2000 pound category, and 16 for the 20000 pound category. Of these 88 regressions, fully 50 (57%) had $R^2$s greater than 0.95 and only 12 (14%) had $R^2$s less than 0.80.

These findings indicated that the rates within a state for a particular weight class tended to follow closely the simple formula depicted in equation (1).[18] We also noted that the formulas across states varied significantly.[19] We concluded that a properly specified empirical model would account for the observed within-state regularities. Thus, we chose not to combine the data from the various states and regress trucking rates on a constant, the distance of the route, and a series of regulatory variables. Doing so would force the constant term and the elasticity of trucking rates with respect to distance to be the same across states, restrictions that do not appear appropriate.

We proceeded as follows. As shown in equation (1), each state "formula" relating rates to mileage contains two parameters: a constant term ($\alpha$) and the elasticity of rates with respect to mileage ($\beta$). We hypothesized that each state's "formula" depended on the cost conditions particular to that state, and on the state's motor carrier regulations. Thus, we modify equation (1) by interacting $\alpha$ and $\beta$ with variables that control for state-specific cost conditions and regulations. Note that this specification is as general as possible: We permit regulations to affect both a state's constant term ($\alpha$) and its elasticity of rates with respect to mileage ($\beta$).[20]

Based on the preceding discussion, the equation we estimate is:

---

[18] In a separate set of analyses, we included as independent variables the populations of the origin and the destination cities, and the population densities of the counties lying between these cities. Including these variables did not increase significantly the explanatory power of the state-specific regressions, and had no meaningful affect on the estimated relationships between intrastate trucking rates and state trucking regulations.

[19] States with a relatively large constant term ($\alpha$) tend to have a relatively small elasticity with respect to mileage ($\beta$) and vice versa.

[20] While we have some *a priori* expectations concerning the direction of the relationships between trucking rates and various regulations, we have none concerning whether these relationships are sensitive to the distance of the route.

$$(2) \quad R_{ijk} = \alpha_0 + \alpha_1 * INDEX_k + \alpha_2 * \mathbf{REG_k} + \beta_0 * M_{ijk} + \beta_1 * M_{ijk} * INDEX_k$$

$$+$$

$$\beta_2 * M_{ijk} * \mathbf{REG_k} + u_{ijk}$$

where,

| | | |
|---|---|---|
| $R_{ijk}$ | = | the log of the rate for route i, weight j, and state k |
| $INDEX_k$ | = | variable measuring state k's cost conditions |
| $\mathbf{REG_k}$ | = | vector of 0-1 dummy variables describing motor carrier regulations in state k |
| $M_{ijk}$ | = | the log of the mileage for route i, weight j, and state k |
| $u_{ijk}$ | = | error term with mean 0 and variance $\sigma^2$ |
| $\alpha$'s, $\beta$'s | = | parameters to be estimated |

and **bold-faced** items represent vectors.

As mentioned above, in this specification the relationship between a particular regulation and rates is a function of mileage.

The variable $INDEX_k$ is intended to capture the cost conditions affecting the trucking industry in state k. In constructing this variable we exploited the fact that our data contain interstate trucking rates as well as intrastate ones. All interstate rates are subject to a common regulatory structure -- the 1980 MCA. Thus, holding distance constant, variations in interstate rates cannot be due to regulatory differences; they must be due instead to differences in local cost conditions, such as labor and fuel costs, congestion costs, and topographical features. We therefore used the interstate rate information to construct a set of state-specific indices reflecting each state's cost conditions.

To compute a particular state's cost index we proceeded as follows. We identified all of the interstate routes in our data that either originated or terminated in the state. Then, for each state, we ran a simple regression akin to equation (1) above: the dependent variable was

30

the log of the interstate rate, and the independent variables were a constant and the log of mileage. The two coefficients generated by such a regression provide a measure of the cost conditions particular to that state; states with higher costs would have larger coefficients. Creating a state specific cost index involved two additional steps. First, we used these coefficients to predict the log of an interstate rate for a route of a distance equal to the average intrastate route in the state. Naturally, states with shorter routes would have lower predicted rates than states with longer ones. To create an index that could be compared across states, we divided each state's predicted rate by the length of the state's average intrastate rate. This normalizes the predicted interstate rate to a "per mile" equivalent (expressed in logs), permitting one to compare meaningfully the index from a small state to one from a larger one.

Prior to presenting the empirical results, we note that our empirical specification in equation (2) treats state-level regulations as exogenous variables. Such an approach would not be proper if regulations and prices are determined simultaneously. It could be the case that the level of prices affects the regulations that exist as well as *vice versa*. If this were the case, then equation 2 would suffer from specification error and the estimated coefficients would be biased.[21]

We believe treating state-level regulations as exogenous does not introduce simultaneity bias for two reasons. First, the troublesome bias discussed above would arise in the following circumstances: suppose that states without regulation contain only a few trucking firms who could effectively collude to raise prices ten percent above competitive

---

[21] Several recent studies of state-level regulations have attempted to correct for the possible simultaneity between prices and regulation. See, for instance, Mathios and Rogers (1989) and Lanning, Morrisey, and Ohsfeldt (1991). For a discussion of recent empirical studies of regulation, see Joskow and Rose (1989) and Klevorick (1991).

levels. Now assume that state regulation in the public interest would only be partially successful, lowering prices to five percent above competitive levels. A naive regression model of this situation could show that regulation raised prices five percent, when in fact it had the opposite effect.

We do not believe that the situations we are examining fit the above circumstances. In that scenario, trucking firms that operate intrastate trucking routes could be expected to oppose state regulation. For the most part, however, intrastate trucking firms support economic regulation, claiming various efficiency grounds. This fact, combined with the generally unconcentrated structure of the industry, lead us to conclude that this type of bias is not a problem here.

Second, our data stem from a cross-section of rates for the spring of 1987.[22] Simultaneity bias would not exist if the regulations at issue were pre-determined, that is, if regulations were affected by *prior* years' rates but not by 1987 rates.[23] Of the thirty-nine states included in the data, the Baker survey indicates that thirty-five did not pass economic motor carrier legislation in 1986 or 1987. We believe that for these states it is reasonable to assume that the state-level regulations in effect during the spring of 1987 were pre-

---

[22] The cross-section nature of our data differs from the time-series data utilized by Lanning *et al.* (1991) in their study of hospital regulations. There, the regulations of interest were imposed in the midst of the time period covered by the data, making endogeneity a serious concern.

[23] States first implemented motor carrier regulations in the first three decades of this century, and most states amended their regulations to make them consistent with the 1935 Motor Carrier Act. It is well accepted that the 1935 Act was implemented, in large measure, to insulate railroads from trucking competition. Between 1940 and 1980, changes in both state-level and federal motor carrier regulations were rare. Since the passage of the 1980 Motor Carrier Act, which deregulated many aspects of interstate trucking, a number of states have reconsidered their motor carrier regulations. Several states amended their regulations in ways similar to the 1980 MCA; a few others deregulated their intrastate motor carrier industries completely. This latter group is not included in our data, because the absence of regulation implies the absence of filed tariffs, which we rely on for our rate data.

determined.[24] The four states that did enact meaningful economic legislation or amend meaningful economic regulations in 1986 or 1987 were California, Colorado, Georgia, and Utah.

In California, the state Public Utility Commission reimposed significant rate regulations in April 1986, including requirements that some rates be raised ten percent on the grounds that overly low rates and profit margins induced truckers to compromise on safety. Throughout 1986 and 1987, motor carrier regulation continued to be debated in California. Still, the April 1986 decisions by the CAPUC were implemented in May 1986, and should have been reflected in the 1987 rates. Thus, we believe it is reasonable to interpret the California regulations as exogenous.

The Baker survey does not provide details on the regulatory and legislative changes that reportedly occurred in Colorado in 1986. Our review of the trade press failed to uncover any mention of any changes. Thus, we assume that these changes were not substantial.

Georgia enacted legislation in 1985 intended to relax its entry requirements for intrastate truckers; this law went into effect on January 1, 1986. The new, more "relaxed", law, however, still required prospective entrants to establish that their entry would fulfill an important public need. While this change could facilitate entry (it is potentially less burdensome that having to show that existing carriers cannot provide adequate service), in our parlance it still qualifies as "somewhat strict" entry requirements. Thus, the change in Georgia does not appear to be a significant one. Further, given its enactment date of January 1, 1986, we believe that the effects of the changes in Georgia's regulatory regime would be incorporated into rates by the spring of 1987.

---

[24] According to the Baker survey, two of these states (ND and SD) enacted partial deregulation in 1985. We assume that by the spring of 1987 the effects of these changes would be fully realized in trucking rates.

Finally, the 1987 Baker survey indicates that in 1986 Utah passed a law similar to the 1980 MCA, and that in 1987 the Utah legislature did not consider further trucking deregulation. As in the other states, we assume that these facts support our contention that the effects of the 1986 changes would have been reflected in 1987 rates.

We conclude, therefore, that the cross-section nature of our study and the relative fixity of state-level regulations concerning the motor carrier industry, permits us to treat state-level motor carrier regulations as exogenous variables.

### C. Estimation Results

We estimated equation 2 separately for each of the three weight classes in our data: less than 500 pounds; 2000 pounds; and 20000 pounds. Initially, all four of the regulatory variables were included as independent variables. To examine whether the effect of a particular regulation depends on the status of the other regulations, we also estimated equation 2 for subsets of the data, determined by the status of a particular regulatory variable. For example, we limited the analysis to those observations where entry regulations are strict.[25] From this analysis we can learn whether the relationship between trucking rates and a particular regulation depends on the status of other regulations.[26]

Table 3 lists the dependent and independent variables included in the analysis; the dependent variable is the log of the intrastate rate. Table 4 contains the means and standard deviations for these variables for each of the three weight categories analyzed.

---

[25] That is, we ran the regression only on those observations where ENTRY1 or ENTRY2 equals one, and dropped ENTRY1 and ENTRY2 as independent variables.

[26] An alternative approach to assessing the magnitude of such interaction effects among the regulatory variables would be to add to equation (2) a series of additional independent variables that interact the various regulatory variables with each other. This approach yields results qualitatively and quantitatively very similar to those reported below.

Table 3

Variables included in the regression analysis

| Variable | Variable description |
| --- | --- |
| LRATE | Log of the intrastate rate, which is expressed in cents per hundred weight for a shipment of a particular weight on a particular route |
| LMILES | Log of the route's distance, in miles |
| LINDEX | Local Cost index -- estimate of the log of the per mile cost of a typical interstate shipment that either originates or terminates in the state |
| RATEREG | dummy variable equal to one if the state strictly regulates motor carrier rates; zero otherwise; |
| ENTRY1 | dummy variable equal to one if the state has strict entry requirements and if protests by incumbent carriers against applications for new entry are very effective; zero otherwise; |
| ENTRY2 | dummy variable equal to one if the state has strict entry requirements and if protests by incumbent carriers against applications for new entry are somewhat effective; zero otherwise; |
| IMMUNE | dummy variable equal to one if the state grants rate bureaus antitrust immunity; zero otherwise; |
| M_LINDEX | LMILES times LINDEX |
| M_RATEREG | LMILES times RATEREG |
| M_ENTRY1 | LMILES times ENTRY1 |
| M_ENTRY2 | LMILES times ENTRY2 |
| M_IMMUNE | LMILES times IMMUNE |

Table 4

**Means and Standard Deviations of Variables**
**Included in the Regression Analysis**
(various weight categories)

| | WEIGHT CATEGORY | | | | | |
|---|---|---|---|---|---|---|
| | < 500 pounds (n=673) | | 2000 pounds (n=644) | | 20000 pounds (n=290) | |
| Variable | Mean | Std. Dev. | Mean | Std. Dev. | Mean | Std. Dev. |
| LRATE | 7.132 | 0.348 | 6.637 | 0.343 | 5.655 | 0.513 |
| LMILES | 5.095 | 0.675 | 5.101 | 0.684 | 5.246 | 0.662 |
| LINDEX | 2.176 | 0.317 | 1.606 | 0.302 | 0.665 | 0.276 |
| RATEREG | 0.489 | 0.500 | 0.475 | 0.500 | 0.634 | 0.482 |
| ENTRY1 | 0.220 | 0.414 | 0.258 | 0.438 | 0.248 | 0.433 |
| ENTRY2 | 0.608 | 0.489 | 0.636 | 0.482 | 0.538 | 0.499 |
| IMMUNE | 0.574 | 0.495 | 0.564 | 0.496 | 0.662 | 0.474 |
| M_LINDEX | 10.949 | 1.288 | 8.063 | 1.167 | 3.389 | 1.089 |
| M_RATEREG | 2.549 | 2.650 | 2.487 | 2.659 | 3.448 | 2.648 |
| M_ENTRY1 | 1.161 | 2.201 | 1.383 | 2.365 | 1.332 | 2.338 |
| M_ENTRY2 | 3.034 | 2.498 | 3.162 | 2.468 | 2.784 | 2.622 |
| M_IMMUNE | 2.970 | 2.614 | 2.928 | 2.630 | 3.611 | 2.612 |

Tables R1 - R3 contain the regression results for the less than 500 pound, 2000 pound, and 20000 pound regressions. The first column of each table includes all four of the regulatory variables as independent variables, and therefore includes all of the observations in the analysis. The other three columns in each table contain the results from running the regression on subsets of the data, where the subsets are determined by the status of a particular regulation. The second column limits the analysis to states where rates are regulated strictly (RATEREG=1); the third column limits the analysis to states where entry is very or somewhat restricted (ENTRY1=1 or ENTRY2=1); and the fourth column is limited to states where rate bureaus are granted antitrust immunity (IMMUNE=1). We use the results from columns (2) through (4) to examine whether the relationship between a particular regulation and trucking rates depends on the status of the other regulations.

## Table R1: Regression Coefficients
### Dependent Variable: Log of intrastate rate

<u>WEIGHT: less than 500 pounds</u>

|  | (1) ALL OBS. | (2) RATEREG=1 | (3) ENTRY1=1 or ENTRY2=1 | (4) IMMUNE=1 |
|---|---|---|---|---|
| LMILES | 0.270*** (0.104) | 0.513*** (0.111) | 0.040 (0.110) | 0.495*** (0.102) |
| LINDEX | 0.414** (0.206) | 0.609*** (0.213) | -0.314 (0.216) | 0.467** (0.232) |
| RATEREG | -0.301 (0.237) | --- | -0.630** (0.255) | -0.240 (0.240) |
| ENTRY1 | -0.222 (0.323) | 0.382 (0.375) | --- | 0.211 (0.396) |
| ENTRY2 | -0.342 (0.213) | 0.811** (0.332) | --- | 0.928*** (0.298) |
| IMMUNE | 0.300 (0.235) | -0.259 (0.375) | 1.029*** (0.253) | --- |
| M_LINDEX | -0.013 (0.044) | -0.087* (0.048) | 0.148*** (0.048) | -0.050 (0.051) |
| M_RATEREG | 0.068 (0.045) | --- | 0.147*** (0.050) | 0.037 (0.047) |
| M_ENTRY1 | 0.085 (0.061) | 0.017 (0.070) | --- | 0.019 (0.074) |
| M_ENTRY2 | 0.119*** (0.042) | -0.047 (0.062) | --- | -0.095* (0.057) |
| M_IMMUNE | -0.026 (0.046) | 0.064 (0.072) | -0.167*** (0.050) | --- |
| CONSTANT | 4.684*** (0.518) | 3.670*** (0.555) | 5.869*** (0.508) | 3.905*** (0.484) |
| Mean Dep Var | 7.132 | 7.210 | 7.167 | 7.206 |
| Adj. $R^2$ | 0.418 | 0.611 | 0.436 | 0.528 |
| No. of obs. | 673 | 329 | 557 | 386 |

Standard errors in parentheses.
*** (**) (*) denotes significance at the 1 (5) (10) percent level.

## Table R2: Regression Coefficients
## Dependent Variable: Log of intrastate rate

### WEIGHT: 2000 pounds

| | (1)<br>ALL<br>OBS. | (2)<br><br>RATEREG=1 | (3)<br>ENTRY1=1 or<br>ENTRY2=1 | (4)<br><br>IMMUNE=1 |
|---|---|---|---|---|
| LMILES | 0.252***<br>(0.089) | 0.481***<br>(0.111) | 0.444***<br>(0.064) | 0.502***<br>(0.091) |
| LINDEX | 0.273<br>(0.204) | 0.744***<br>(0.208) | 0.332**<br>(0.166) | 0.607***<br>(0.214) |
| RATEREG | -0.102<br>(0.227) | --- | -0.502**<br>(0.219) | -0.772***<br>(0.279) |
| ENTRY1 | -0.940***<br>(0.325) | -0.346<br>(0.269) | --- | 0.448<br>(0.502) |
| ENTRY2 | -0.545**<br>(0.223) | DD | --- | 1.163***<br>(0.419) |
| IMMUNE | 0.435**<br>(0.207) | -0.323<br>(0.367) | 0.907***<br>(0.217) | --- |
| M_LINDEX | 0.002<br>(0.042) | -0.109**<br>(0.045) | -0.011<br>(0.035) | -0.068<br>(0.045) |
| M_RATEREG | 0.040<br>(0.044) | --- | 0.118***<br>(0.043) | 0.162***<br>(0.056) |
| M_ENTRY1 | 0.218***<br>(0.063) | 0.071<br>(0.050) | --- | -0.037<br>(0.095) |
| M_ENTRY2 | 0.143***<br>(0.044) | DD | --- | -0.169**<br>(0.080) |
| M_IMMUNE | -0.062<br>(0.041) | 0.074<br>(0.070) | -0.153***<br>(0.043) | --- |
| CONSTANT | 4.613***<br>(0.445) | 3.906***<br>(0.549) | 3.826***<br>(0.316) | 3.399***<br>(0.468) |
| | | | | |
| Mean Dep Var | 6.636 | 6.768 | 6.661 | 6.719 |
| Adj. $R^2$ | 0.565 | 0.558 | 0.565 | 0.573 |
| No. of obs. | 644 | 306 | 574 | 363 |

DD : variable dropped due to perfect collinearity.

Standard errors in parentheses.

*** (**) (*) denotes significance at the 1 (5) (10) percent level.

## Table R3:Regression Coefficients
## Dependent Variable: Log of intrastate rate

### WEIGHT: 20000 pounds

| | (1)<br>ALL<br>OBS. | (2)<br><br>RATEREG=1 | (3)<br>ENTRY1=1 or<br>ENTRY2=1 | (4)<br><br>IMMUNE=1 |
|---|---|---|---|---|
| LMILES | -0.221<br>(0.137) | 1.569***<br>(0.344) | 0.166<br>(0.124) | 1.832***<br>(0.368) |
| LINDEX | -2.260***<br>(0.640) | 13.677***<br>(2.920) | -2.714***<br>(0.630) | 12.774***<br>(2.992) |
| RATEREG | 0.151<br>(0.471) | --- | -0.517<br>(0.628) | 1.278**<br>(0.628) |
| ENTRY1 | -2.463***<br>(0.482) | -1.474<br>(0.925) | --- | -2.749***<br>(0.872) |
| ENTRY2 | -1.847***<br>(0.328) | 0.630<br>(0.842) | --- | -0.246<br>(0.680) |
| IMMUNE | -1.246**<br>(0.520) | -0.544<br>(0.585) | 0.075<br>(0.613) | --- |
| M_LINDEX | 0.449***<br>(0.126) | -1.976***<br>(0.539) | 0.588***<br>(0.135) | -2.097***<br>(0.544) |
| M_RATEREG | 0.024<br>(0.089) | --- | 0.159<br>(0.121) | -0.190<br>(0.116) |
| M_ENTRY1 | 0.474***<br>(0.090) | 0.301*<br>(0.161) | --- | 0.521***<br>(0.156) |
| M_ENTRY2 | 0.340***<br>(0.062) | -0.074<br>(0.143) | --- | 0.069<br>(0.119) |
| M_IMMUNE | 0.230<br>(0.099) | 0.098<br>(0.112) | -0.035<br>(0.117) | --- |
| CONSTANT | 6.637<br>(0.726) | -4.561**<br>(1.896) | 4.441***<br>(0.653) | -5.248**<br>(2.031) |
| Mean Dep Var | 5.655 | 5.851 | 5.664 | 5.777 |
| Adj. $R^2$ | 0.676 | 0.742 | 0.680 | 0.585 |
| No. of obs. | 290 | 184 | 228 | 192 |

Standard errors in parentheses.
*** (**) (*) denotes significance at the 1 (5) (10) percent level.

Two issues arise in using the results in Tables R1 - R3 to generate estimates of the relationships between trucking regulations and trucking rates. First, the dependent variable is the log of the intrastate rate, and the regulatory variables are 0-1 dummy variables. In such circumstances, the expression for the percentage change in the dependent variable associated with the dummy variable is $e^{\beta} - 1$, where $\beta$ is the estimated coefficient on the dummy variable. Second, in our empirical specification, the relationship between trucking regulations and trucking rates is a function of mileage, which means that there is no single value for the relationship between a regulation and trucking rates. Rather, the relationship will depend on the length of the route.[27]

We use the results from the regressions to examine the relationships between various trucking regulations and trucking rates. The results from the two LTL regressions are very similar, but differ somewhat from those from the TL regression. We therefore first discuss the LTL results and then move on to the TL results.

### 1. LTL Regressions (weight = <500 and 2000 pounds)

As explained above, in our specification the relationship between trucking rates and a particular regulation is a function of the distance of the route. Two coefficients from the regression results must be combined to generate estimates of the relationships between trucking rates and trucking regulations. Tables E1 and E2 contain the estimated percentage changes in trucking rates associated with various state-level motor carrier regulations for the

---

[27] Suppose one were interested in the percentage difference in trucking rates in states that strictly regulate trucking rates compared to rates in states that do not strictly regulate trucking rates, for a shipment of less than 500 pounds on a 200 mile route. Looking at column (1) of Table R1, one would first add the coefficient on the variable RATEREG to the product of the log of 200 times the coefficient on the variable M_RATEREG. The value of this expression is: $-0.301 + \log(200) * 0.068 = 0.0593$. The percentage increase in trucking rates associated with the presence of strict rate regulation for a less than 500 pound shipment on a 200 mile route would then be $e^{.0593} - 1 = .0611$, or 6.11 percent.

two LTL weights.   Each of these tables provides the estimated relationship between regulations and rates for three different mileages - the 25th percentile mileage of the routes included in the analysis, the median mileage, and the 75th percentile mileage.[28]

---

[28] Tables E1 and E2 rely on column (1) from the regression results.  Thus, they represent the average relationship between trucking rates and the various trucking regulations, holding the other regulations constant.  Later, we will present and discuss results based on columns (2) through (4) of the regression results, which permit the relationship between a regulation and rates to depend on which other regulations pertain in the state.

## Table E1

### Average Percentage Change in Intrastate Trucking Rates Associated with Various Motor Carrier Regulations

| | WEIGHT = less than 500 pounds | | |
|---|---|---|---|
| | 25th Percentile Mileage (110) | Median Mileage (178) | 75th Percentile Mileage (271) |
| **Regulation** | | | |
| Strict Rate Regulation (RATEREG=1) | 1.72% (3.23) | 5.09%* (2.66) | 8.12%** (3.47) |
| Very Strict Entry Regul. (ENTRY1=1) | 19.54%*** (5.14) | 24.55%*** (3.93) | 29.10%*** (4.49) |
| Somewhat Strict Entry Regul. (ENTRY2=1) | 24.43%*** (3.44) | 31.78%*** (3.13) | 38.55%*** (3.81) |
| Antitrust Immunity for Rate Bureaus (IMMUNE=1) | 19.58%*** (3.05) | 18.10%*** (2.65) | 16.83%*** (3.63) |

Standard errors in parentheses.
*** (**) (*) denotes significance at the 1 (5) (10) percent level.

Source:  Calculated from results of regression (1), Table R1

43

## Table E2

### Average Percentage Change in Intrastate Trucking Rates Associated with Various Motor Carrier Regulations

| | WEIGHT = 2000 pounds | | |
|---|---|---|---|
| | 25th Percentile Mileage (110) | Median Mileage (181) | 75th Percentile Mileage (277) |
| **Regulation** | | | |
| Strict Rate Regulation (RATEREG=1) | 9.10%*** (2.94) | 11.32%*** (2.53) | 13.24%*** (3.50) |
| Very Strict Entry Regul. (ENTRY1=1) | 8.58% (5.05) | 21.00%*** (4.27) | 32.69%*** (5.24) |
| Somewhat Strict Entry Regul. (ENTRY2=1) | 13.77%*** (3.57) | 22.18%*** (3.53) | 29.84%*** (4.47) |
| Antitrust Immunity for Rate Bureaus (IMMUNE=1) | 15.55%*** (2.59) | 12.05%*** (2.38) | 9.15%*** (3.36) |

Standard errors in parentheses.
*** (**) (*) denotes significance at the 1 (5) (10) percent level.

Source: Calculated from results of regression (1), Table R2

Tables E1 and E2 indicate that the four regulatory variables are positively and statistically significantly related to LTL trucking rates, with entry restrictions having the largest effect. These findings are consistent with our *a priori* expectations.

Looking at the median length route, very strict entry requirements raise LTL trucking rates between 21 and 25 percent, and somewhat strict entry requirements raise LTL rates between 22 and 32 percent.[29] Antitrust immunity for rate bureaus increases LTL trucking rates between 12 and 18 percent, and strict rate regulation increases LTL rates by between 5 and 11 percent.

These general conclusions hold up for the other two mileages analyzed, the 25th and 75th percentile mileages. In these analyses, all four of the regulations are positively related to trucking rates, and the largest effect stems from entry regulations.[30]

As described earlier, our statistical formulation permits the effect of a regulation to be a function of mileage. In the LTL analysis, the only type of regulation that displayed a significant mileage effect was entry regulation. The first column of tables R1 and R2 indicates that the positive relationship between entry restrictions and trucking rates increases with mileage.[31] Two explanations can be offered to explain this result. First, in a given state, obtaining authority to serve a longer route may be more difficult than obtaining

---

[29] We had expected ENTRY1 to increase trucking rates more than ENTRY2 because ENTRY1 represents more stringent entry requirements. We found, however, the opposite pattern for the median length route: ENTRY2 increased trucking rates more than ENTRY1. At the median mileages, however, the differences are not statistically significant in the 2000 pound analysis, though they are significant at the 10% level in the less than 500 pound analysis.

[30] Although all of the estimated relationships are positive, 2 of the 24 coefficients presented in Tables E1 and E2 are not significant at standard levels.

[31] Note the positive significant coefficient on M_ENTRY2 in the less than 500 pound regression, and the positive significant coefficients on M_ENTRY1 and M_ENTRY2 in the 2000 pound regression.

authority to serve a shorter one. This might arise because relatively longer routes typically include a number of shorter routes along the way. Thus, a motor carrier requesting authority to serve a relatively longer route may need to engage in more complex discussions with the regulatory agency, and may be more likely to confront protests by incumbent carriers seeking to delay or prevent the granting of the authority. Second, the shorter routes in our sample tend to arise in relatively smaller states, *i.e.*, ones that can be served relatively easily with interstate shipments from neighboring states. Consequently, restricting entry into relatively short intrastate routes may tend to have a relatively smaller impact on rates than restricting entry into relatively long ones, where interstate shipments do not provide as viable a competitive threat.

Next, we examine whether the relationship between a particular regulation and trucking rates depends on the status of the other regulations. For this, we use the results from columns (2) - (4) of Tables R1 and R2. As before, the relationship between a particular regulation and trucking rates is a function of mileage, so the coefficients in the regression tables by themselves do not provide sufficient information to determine these relationships.

We use the coefficients from the regression tables to compute the percentage changes in trucking rates associated with various regulations depending on the status of the other regulations; the results are contained in Tables S1 and S2.

## Table S1

## Percentage Change in Intrastate Trucking Rates
## Associated with Various Motor Carrier Regulations
## Depending on the Status of Other Regulations

WEIGHT = less than 500 pounds
(mileage = median mileage of 178 miles)

| Regulation | RATEREG=1 (n=329) | ENTRY1=1 or ENTRY2=1 (n=557) | IMMUNE=1 (n=386) |
|---|---|---|---|
| Strict Rate Regulation (RATEREG=1) | ---- | 14.26%*** (2.99) | -4.84% (3.13) |
| Very Strict Entry Regul. (ENTRY1=1) | 60.24%*** (4.27) | ---- | 36.41%*** (4.46) |
| Somewhat Strict Entry Regul. (ENTRY2=1) | 76.49%*** (3.96) | ---- | 54.83%*** (3.58) |
| Antitrust Immunity for Rate Bureaus (IMMUNE=1) | 7.62%** (3.11) | 17.50%*** (2.71) | ---- |

Standard errors in parentheses.
*** (**) (*) denotes significance at the 1 (5) (10) percent level.

Source: Calculated from regressions (2), (3), and (4) in Table R1

## Table S2

### Percentage Change in Intrastate Trucking Rates Associated with Various Motor Carrier Regulations Depending on the Status of Other Regulations

WEIGHT = 2000 pounds
(mileage = median mileage of 181 miles)

| | RATEREG=1 (n=306) | ENTRY1=1 or ENTRY2=1 (n=574) | IMMUNE=1 (n=363) |
|---|---|---|---|
| **Regulation** | | | |
| Strict Rate Regulation (RATEREG=1) | ---- | 11.59%*** (2.51) | 7.30%** (3.51) |
| Very Strict Entry Regul. (ENTRY1=1) | 2.22% (2.78) | ---- | 29.46%*** (5.55) |
| Somewhat Strict Entry Regul. (ENTRY2=1) | n/a | ---- | 32.92%*** (4.64) |
| Antitrust Immunity for Rate Bureaus (IMMUNE=1) | 6.52%** (3.11) | 11.84%*** (2.29) | ---- |

Standard errors in parentheses.
*** (**) (*) denotes significance at the 1 (5) (10) percent level.

Source: Calculated from regressions (2), (3), and (4) in Table R2

The basic message from Tables S1 and S2 is that interaction effects are important in determining the magnitude of a regulation's relationship with trucking rates, but they do not alter the basic finding that each of these regulations tends to be associated with higher trucking rates. Particularly noteworthy is the increase in the effect on rates from entry regulations when the analysis is limited to states where rate bureaus are provided antitrust immunity (IMMUNE=1). In the LTL analyses, the percentage increase in rates when strict entry controls exist increases to the neighborhood of 30 to 55 percent when the analysis is limited to such states. This result squares with expectations: the positive effect of entry regulation on rates is even more pronounced when rate bureaus provide immunity for jointly coordinated activities.

To examine whether the generally positive relationship between strict entry regulations and trucking rates also held in states that did not offer antitrust immunity to rate bureaus, we conducted (but do not report the results here) a separate analysis for states that did not offer antitrust immunity for rate bureaus (*i.e.*, states in which IMMUNE=0). In this analysis, the relationship between trucking rates and entry controls remained positive and statistically different from zero at the median mileage distances. From these results we conclude that strict entry restrictions, by themselves, contribute to higher trucking rates, and that this positive effect is strengthened when entry controls are combined with the provision of antitrust immunity for rate bureaus.

In a similar vein, Tables S1 and S2 indicate that the positive relationship between antitrust immunity and trucking rates is greater in those states where entry regulations are very or somewhat strict (ENTRY1=1 or ENTRY2=1). This confirms that the generally positive relationship between antitrust immunity and trucking rates is driven by states that combine antitrust immunity with strict entry requirements.

Finally, note that in the less than 500 pound analysis entry restrictions tend to increase rates in the neighborhood of 60 percent to 75 percent in states that also impose strict rate regulation. This finding indicates that some rates are particularly high where states not only regulate rates, but also restrict entry, thereby deterring firms from serving potentially profitable routes. This entry barrier permits the firms already operating to retain the rents created by the regulated rates.[32]

In sum, three basic findings emerge from the LTL regressions. First, the three types of state trucking regulations examined in this study clearly affect LTL trucking rates. On average, each is positively and significantly related to LTL trucking rates.[33]

Second, the positive relationship between strict entry requirements and trucking rates is particularly strong in states that also grant antitrust immunity to rate bureaus; in such states, strict entry requirements drive up intrastate trucking rates in the neighborhood of 30 percent to 55 percent. In the less than 500 pound analysis, we also found that the positive relationship between strict entry restrictions and rates increases markedly in states that

---

[32] We find it interesting that practically every state with strict rate regulation also had strict entry controls. Of the 20 states with strict rate regulation, 18 also had somewhat or very strict entry restrictions. In fact, in the 2000 pound analysis, *every* state with strict rate regulation (RATEREG = 1) also had either very or somewhat strict entry restrictions (ENTRY1 = 1 or ENTRY2 = 1).

[33] Recall that we discounted the intrastate rates according to the discounts typically offered by carriers in the state. While we believe it is important to account for such discounting given the prevalence of the practice, we nonetheless reran the LTL regressions using the undiscounted rate data. In these analyses, the positive relationships between trucking rates and rate regulation and entry regulation diminished in magnitude relative to those reported in the text, and in some instances the relationships even became negative. These results confirm the importance of accounting for discounting, and demonstrate that failing to do so (*i.e.*, relying solely on filed tariffs) could lead to incorrect inferences concerning the relationships between trucking rates and regulations.

regulate rates strictly.[34] These findings provide strong support for relaxing entry restrictions generally, especially in states that also grant antitrust immunity to rate bureaus or regulate rate levels.

Third, the generally positive and significant coefficient on RATEREG indicates that strict regulation of rates by state authorities does tends to raise trucking rates. On the other hand, the combination of strict rate regulation and rate bureau antitrust immunity has, on balance, a negative effect on LTL trucking rates.[35]

### 2. TL Regression (weight = 20000)

Before discussing the TL results, we should note that we place relatively less weight on the results from the TL analysis compared to those from the LTL analysis. Recall that our rate data contain common carrier class rates. Unlike LTL shipments, TL common carrier shipments are typically transported under commodity, not class rates. Thus, class rates may be relatively poorer measures of TL shipment rates than they are of LTL rates.

Table E3 contains the average percentage change in 20000 pound trucking rates associated with particular regulations for three mileage levels; these figures rely on the coefficients from the first column of Table R3. The results from the TL analysis (20000 pounds) differ somewhat from those discussed above for the LTL regressions.

---

[34] In the 2000 pound analysis, collinearity among the regulatory variables prevented determining how entry regulations affected rates in states that also strictly regulate their rates.

[35] As a check on these findings given the possible endogeneity between trucking rates and trucking regulations, we conducted the statistical analysis after deleting observations from the four states where trucking regulations changed in 1986 (CA, CO, GA, UT). In the LTL analysis, the basic findings discussed above were not altered when these four states were deleted.

51

## Table E3

### Average Percentage Change in Intrastate Trucking Rates Associated with Various Motor Carrier Regulations

| | WEIGHT = 20000 pounds | | |
|---|---|---|---|
| | 25th Percentile Mileage (137) | Median Mileage (214) | 75th Percentile Mileage (304) |
| **Regulation** | | | |
| Strict Rate Regulation (RATEREG=1) | 31.15%*** (5.70) | 32.58%*** (4.64) | 33.72%*** (5.90) |
| Very Strict Entry Regul. (ENTRY1=1) | -12.22%* (7.03) | 8.44% (6.05) | 28.07%*** (6.70) |
| Somewhat Strict Entry Regul. (ENTRY2=1) | -15.94%*** (5.37) | -2.18% (5.11) | 10.22 (5.89) |
| Antitrust Immunity for Rate Bureaus (IMMUNE=1) | -10.68%** (5.57) | -1.02% (5.01) | 7.31% (6.93) |

Standard errors in parentheses.
*** (**) (*) denotes significance at the 1 (5) (10) percent level.

Source: Calculated from results of regression (1), Table R3

Perhaps the most surprising result from Table E3 is that the positive relationship between entry restrictions and trucking rates that was so evident in the LTL analysis is not present in this TL analysis. At the median mileage distance, neither of the two entry regulation variables have a statistically significant relationship with trucking rates. In fact, the relationship between trucking rates and entry restrictions is negative at short distances, and becomes positive only for relatively longer routes. Note, however, that the (unexpected) negative relationship between entry restrictions and rates arises on short, TL routes -- ones that would appear to be the exception rather than the rule in most trucking markets. Thus, we do not believe that these findings weaken significantly the general finding from the LTL regressions, and from the results from relatively long TL routes, that entry restrictions tend to increase trucking rates.

The first row of Table E3 indicates that TL trucking rates are significantly higher -- over 30 percent -- in states that strictly regulate trucking rates, and that this relationship is insensitive to the distance of the route. This latter finding is consistent with that found in the LTL analysis that strict rate regulation tends to contribute to higher trucking rates.

Table E3 also indicates that, at the median distance in the TL analysis, there is no significant relationship between antitrust immunity and motor carrier rates. While at shorter distances the relationship is negative, we noted above that such routes -- short, TL ones -- would appear to be rare. Thus, as with the entry results discussed above, these results seem too weak to alter the basic conclusion reached in the LTL analysis that the provision of antitrust immunity tends to increase trucking rates.[36]

---

[36] As in the LTL analysis, we reran the TL regressions using undiscounted rate data. Two significant differences emerged from those reported in the text: the positive relationship between rate regulation and TL rates diminished in magnitude (though it remained statitistically significant) and the relationship between TL rates and entry restrictions became

(continued...)

Table S3 contains the results from running the TL regression on subsets of the data depending on the status of other regulatory variables. In these regressions, the general finding that entry restrictions, when combined with other regulations, increase rates tends to reemerge. In particular, note the positive and significant coefficients on the ENTRY2 variable. This suggests that in the TL sector, as in the LTL sector, the combination of entry restrictions and either antitrust immunity or strict rate regulation contributes to higher trucking rates.

The first row of Table S3 indicates that the strong positive relationship between strict rate regulation and trucking rates arises in states that either restrict entry or that provide antitrust immunity to rate bureaus. Finally, the last row of Table S3 provides some support for the proposition that the provision of antitrust immunity helps to reduce TL trucking rates in states where entry requirements are somewhat or very strict. We do not place considerable weight on this finding because any efficiencies should be more likely to arise in LTL shipments, not TL ones, and the LTL analysis consistently concluded that antitrust immunity was associated with increased trucking rates.[37]

---

[36](...continued)
negative and significant. We conclude from these results, as we did from the LTL ones, that relying on undiscounted rate data could lead to incorrect inferences concerning the relationships between trucking rates and regulations.

[37] As in the LTL analysis, we reran the TL regressions after deleting observations from the states where were trucking regulations were changed in 1986. After deleting these observations, the relationship between entry restrictions and trucking rates was either insignificantly different from zero or negative, the positive relationship between strict rate regulation and rates increased in magnitude, and the relationship between trucking rates and the provision of antitrust immunity remained insignificantly different from zero. The only puzzling aspect of these findings is the sometimes negative relationship between entry restrictions and shipping rates. As noted in the text, we place less weight in the findings from the TL analysis than in those from the LTL analyses.

**Percentage Change in Intrastate Trucking Rates
Associated with Various Motor Carrier Regulations
Depending on the Status of Other Regulations**

WEIGHT = 20000 pounds
(mileage = median mileage of 214 miles)

| | RATEREG=1 (n=184) | ENTRY1=1 or ENTRY2=1 (n=228) | IMMUNE=1 (n=192) |
|---|---|---|---|
| **Regulation** | | | |
| Strict Rate Regulation (RATEREG=1) | ---- | 40.07%*** (6.19) | 29.26%*** (6.01) |
| Very Strict Entry Regul. (ENTRY1=1) | 15.27% (9.96) | ---- | 5.04% (8.98) |
| Somewhat Strict Entry Regul. (ENTRY2=1) | 26.20%*** (9.51) | ---- | 13.01%* (7.32) |
| Antitrust Immunity for Rate Bureaus (IMMUNE=1) | -2.07% (4.78) | -10.82%** (5.49) | ---- |

Standard errors in parentheses.
*** (**) (*) denotes significance at the 1 (5) (10) percent level.

Source: Calculated from regressions (2), (3), and (4) in Table R3

## V. Conclusion

In this study, we have sought to disentangle the effects on trucking rates from various types of trucking regulation imposed at the state-level. To do so, we have characterized state-level regulations by a series of attributes, rather than merely a single 0-1 variable as in many regulation studies. While the empirical results vary to some extent depending on the particular weight category examined, some important regularities emerged from this analysis.

The LTL results strongly indicate that each of the regulations considered in this study -- rate regulation, entry regulation, and the provision of antitrust immunity for decisions made jointly -- are positively related to trucking rates. In other words, the familiar finding that trucking regulation increases trucking rates can apparently be extended to each of these three regulatory components. Given the prevalence of LTL shipments in intrastate trucking, deregulating even a portion of a state's regulatory apparatus would appear likely to benefit that state's consumers and shippers by lowering LTL shipping rates. In the TL sector, our analysis indicates that rate regulation increases rates considerably, but that the relationships between trucking rates and the other two types of regulations are less significant.

Both the LTL and TL results indicate that combining entry regulations with either strict rate regulation or state-level antitrust immunity contributes to significantly higher trucking rates. Based on this finding, we believe that significant reductions in trucking rates could occur if states with multiple forms of economic regulation started by loosening their restrictions on entry.

With respect to the regulation of trucking rates, our analysis reveals a positive relationship between trucking rates and regulations that strictly regulate them, and this positive effect tends to be enhanced in states that also restrict entry. These findings suggest that state legislators and regulators should give serious consideration to the argument that an unfettered market serves as an effective regulator of trucking rates. Studies at the federal level have identified significant rate declines following the removal of federal rate setting and entry restricting powers, and our results provide support for the same prospects at the state level.

We were particularly interested in examining the relationship between the provision of antitrust immunity and trucking rates. Such immunity is granted in a high percentage of states as well as at the federal level for some rate bureau activities and calls for the removal or extension of this immunity periodically surface. For LTL shipments, we conclude that, on average, there is a significant positive relationship between the provision of antitrust immunity and trucking rates.[38] This finding casts doubt on the proposition that common carrier rate bureaus should be provided antitrust immunity to permit them to coordinate their rates and schedules, and that any cost savings would likely be passed on to shippers in the form of lower rates. To the contrary, the finding suggests that antitrust immunity facilitates rate increases, not cost reductions, among motor carriers.

---

[38] In the TL analysis, the positive relationship between trucking rates and the provision of antitrust immunity does not arise.

## APPENDIX A

### The Baker Survey

The 1987 Baker survey covered a number of topics, including entry requirements, the extent to which the state regulates rates, whether the state permits motor carrier rate bureaus to operate in the state and, if so, whether the bureaus enjoy antitrust immunity. The survey is sent to several individuals in each state familiar with the relevant state laws and regulations. Once the initial responses are compiled, a preliminary table is distributed to the respondents for verification. Any comments on the preliminary table are incorporated into the final survey table.[39]

Because the Baker survey was sent to multiple individuals in each state, conflicting responses did occasionally arise.[40] To resolve these discrepancies, we reviewed the responses from the 1986 Baker survey. If only one response were listed in the final 1986 Baker survey, and if this response matched one of the responses listed in the final 1987 survey, and if the state did not alter its motor carrier regulations between 1986 and 1987, then we assumed that the 1986 response also applied to 1987.

This approach resolved all of the discrepancies save one: the responses to the question regarding entry conditions in California. One respondent to the 1987 survey

---

[39] Mr. Baker describes the survey procedure as follows: "Generally, it consisted of distributing questionnaires to and seeking information from persons, agencies and organizations which are eminently qualified and have direct knowledge of the governing motor carrier laws, regulations and policies of the states. In addition, the committee conducts a constant review and study of the activities and policies of the legislatures and regulatory agencies of the respective states. Information from these sources was utilized to prepare a preliminary annual summary which was sent to the participants in this study for verification and any recommended changes."

[40] These conflicts were reported in the final survey table. This study uses the responses to four of the questions included in the Baker survey for each of thirty-nine states. Out of a total of 156 responses, the final 1987 survey reports 12 (7.7%) conflicts.

indicated that entry conditions in California in 1987 were relatively easy; the other respondent indicated that entry conditions were difficult. (The same conflicting responses arose in the 1986 survey.) We decided to characterize California's entry conditions as easy based on a 1988 Report on the California trucking industry submitted to the California Public Utilities Commission by its Strategic Planning Division. According to this report, "entry requirements have never been strict."[41]

---

[41] See California Public Utilities Commission (1988), page 11.

# SUMMARY OF THE MOTOR CARRIER REGULATIONS
## IN THE RESPECTIVE STATES OF THE UNITED STATES

| State | (1) Are motor carriers regulated by the state? | (2) What is the degree of regulation of motor carriers by state? | (3) Has motor carrier deregulation legislation considered during 1986 legislative session? | (4) Has any motor carrier deregulation legislation been proposed during the 1987 session? | (5) What is required to obtain motor common carrier authority from the state? | (6) What is required to obtain motor contract carrier authority from the state? | (7) How effective are protests to motor common carrier applications? | (8) Have certain commodities been made exempt from regulation in the past two years? | (9) To what extent does the state regulate motor common carrier rates? | (10) Do tariff bureaus publish motor carrier rates and dues antitrust immunity exist? | (11) Has sunsetting of the state regulatory commission been considered? | (12) What interest have shippers, politicians, etc shown in motor carrier deregulation? |
|---|---|---|---|---|---|---|---|---|---|---|---|---|
| Alabama | X | A/F | E | E | A | A | A | D | A | B | D | C |
| Alaska | O | C/86² | - | - | - | - | - | - | - | B | - | - |
| Arizona | O | C/81 | - | - | - | - | - | - | - | B | - | - |
| Arkansas | X | E | E | D | A | A | B | B | B | B | D | C |
| California | X | A/E² | E | B | A/E | B/C | D | D | A | A | D | B |
| Colorado | X | A/F | B | E | A | A | B | B | B | B | D | C |
| Connecticut | X | A/E | E | E | A | A | B | D | B | B | D | C |
| Delaware | O³ | . | - | - | - | - | - | - | - | B | - | - |
| Florida | O | C/80 | - | - | - | - | - | - | D | B | - | - |
| Georgia | X | F | B | E | A/B | A | A/B | B | A | A | D | B |
| Hawaii | X | A/E | E | E | A | A | B | D | A | A | D | C |
| Idaho | X | B/D | E | E | A/E | C | C | B | B | A | D | C |
| Illinois | X | A/F | E | E | A | A | B | B | A | A | D | C |
| Indiana | X | A/E | D | D | A | A | B | D | C | B | B⁴ | B/D |
| Iowa | X | E | E | E | A | C | B | D | B | B | C | C |
| Kansas | X | D | E | E | C | C | C | D | B | A | C | C |
| Kentucky | X | A | E | E | A | A | B | D | B | A | D | C |
| Louisiana | X | A | E | E | A | A | A | D | A | B | D | C |
| Maine | O | C/82 | - | - | - | - | - | - | - | B | - | - |
| Maryland | X | B | E | E | A | A | D | D | C | B | D | C |

NOTES:
(1) Year deregulation legislation enacted
(2) Keys A and E
(3) Delaware never regulated general freight motor carriers -- regulates passenger carriers
(4) Indiana legislation to sunset PUC 6-30-88 enacted
(5) New Jersey never regulated general freight motor carriers but regulates passenger, household goods, garbage and bulk commodities motor carriers
(6) Fitness only and no public convenience and necessity

| State | (1) Are motor carriers regulated by the state? | (2) What is the degree of regulation of motor carriers by state? | (3) Was motor carrier deregulation legislation considered during 1986 legislative session? | (4) Has any motor carrier deregulation legislation been proposed during the 1987 session? | (5) What is required to obtain motor common carrier authority from the state? | (6) What is required to obtain motor contract carrier authority from the state? | (7) How effective are protests to motor common carrier applications? | (8) Have certain commodities been made exempt from regulation in the past two years? | (9) To what extent does the state regulate motor common carrier rates? | (10) Do tariff increase public motor carrier rates and dues automatically? | (11) Has sunsetting of the state regulatory commission been considered? | (12) What interest have shippers, politicians, etc shown in motor carrier deregulation? |
|---|---|---|---|---|---|---|---|---|---|---|---|---|
| Massachusetts | X | A | E | E | A | A | B | D | C | A | D | C |
| Michigan | X | A/F | E | E | B | B | B | D | A | A | D | B |
| Minnesota | X | A | E | E | A | A | B | D | C | A | D | C |
| Mississippi | X | A | E | D | A | A | B | D | A | B | D | B |
| Missouri | X | A/F | E | E | A/C | A | B | D | A | A | D | C |
| Montana | X | A/F | E | E | A | B | B | D | A | A | C | C |
| Nebraska | X | A/F | E | E | A | A | A/B | D | A | A | D | B/C |
| Nevada | X | A/F | E | (D/F | A/B | A/B | A/B | D | A | A | D | C |
| New Hampshire | X | A | E | E | A | A | B | D | C | B | D | C |
| New Jersey | O5 | - | E | E | E | - | D | D | D | B | D | - |
| New Mexico | X | A | E | E | A | B | B | D | A | A | C | C |
| New York | X | A/E | E | E | A/D | B/C | C | D | B | A | C | C |
| North Carolina | X | A | E | E | A | A | A | D | A | A | D | C |
| North Dakota | X | E | E | E | A | B | B | D | C | B | D | C |
| Ohio | X | A/F | E | E | A | A | A | D | C | B | D | B |
| Oklahoma | X | A/F | E | E | A | A | A | D | A | A | D | C/D |
| Oregon | X | A | E | E | A | A | A | B | A | A | D | C |
| Pennsylvania | X | A/E | E | E | A/C | A/B | B | D | A | A | D | B |
| Rhode Island | X | A | E | E | A | A | B | D | A | A | C | C |
| South Carolina | X | A/D | E | E | , D | C | B | B | A | A | D | C |

NOTES:
(1) Year deregulation legislation enacted
(2) Keys A and E
(3) Delaware never regulated general freight motor carriers -- regulates passenger carriers
(4) Indiana legislation to sunset PUC 6-30-88 enacted
(5) New Jersey never regulated general freight motor carriers but regulates passenger, household goods, garbage and bulk commodities motor carriers
(6) Fitness only and no public convenience and necessity

61

| State | (1) Are motor carriers regulated by the state? | (2) What is the degree of regulation of motor carriers by state? | (3) Was motor carrier deregulation legislation considered during 1986 legislative session? | (4) Has any motor carrier deregulation legislation been proposed during the 1987 session? | (5) What is required to obtain motor common carrier authority from the state? | (6) What is required to obtain motor contract carrier authority from the state? | (7) How effective are protests to motor common carrier applications? | (8) Have certain commodities been made exempt from regulation in the past two years? | (9) To what extent does the state regulate motor common carrier rates? | (10) Do tariff bureaus publish motor carrier rates and does antitrust immunity exist? | (11) Has supporting of the state regulatory Commission been consolidated? | (12) What interest have shippers, politicians, etc. shown in motor carrier deregulation? |
|---|---|---|---|---|---|---|---|---|---|---|---|---|
| South Dakota | X | A/E | E | E | B | C | B | D | B | B | D | C |
| Tennessee | X | A/E | E | E | A | A | A | D | B | B | D | C |
| Texas | X | A/F | E | D | A | A | A | B | A | A | C | B |
| Utah | X | B/D | A/B | E | D | B | C/D | D | B | B | D | C |
| Vermont | X | B | E | E | D | D | D | D | D | B | D | C |
| Virginia | X | E/F | E | E | A | C | B | D | B'C | A | C | C |
| Washington | X | A | C | C | A | A | A | D | A | B | D | B |
| West Virginia | X | A | E | E | A | A | B | D | A | A | E | C |
| Wisconsin | X0 /X3 | B | E | E | C[6] | C[6] | - | D | D | D | D | C |
| Wyoming | X | A | E | E | A | A/C | A/B | D | A:B | A | D | C |

NOTES: (1) Year deregulation legislation enacted
(2) Keys A and E
(3) Delaware never regulated general freight motor carriers -- regulates passenger carriers
(4) Indiana legislation to sunset PUC 6-30-88 enacted
(5) New Jersey never regulated general freight motor carriers but regulates passenger, household goods, garbage and bulk commodities motor carriers
(6) Fitness only and no public convenience and necessity

## KEYS TO TWELVE SUBJECTS
### INCLUDED IN QUESTIONNAIRE AND SUMMARY

1. Are motor carriers regulated by state?

   (X) Motor carriers are regulated.
   (O) Motor carriers are not regulated.

2. Degree of regulation of motor carriers by state.

   (A) State law provides for full regulation.
   (B) State law enacted provides for partial reregulation.
   (C) Law was passed completely deregulating motor carriers.
   (D) State Commission follows a very liberal regulatory policy.
   (E) State Commission follows a moderately liberal regulatory policy.
   (F) State Commission strictly regulates its motor carriers.

3. Deregulation legislation considered during 1986 legislative session.

   (A) Considered and enacted into law.
   (B) Partial deregulation law enacted.
   (C) Introduced but no Committee vote.
   (D) Law considered and defeated.
   (E) None was considered.
   (F) Regulation increased.

4. Has any deregulation legislation been proposed during the 1987 legislative session?

   (A) Considered and enacted in law.
   (B) Partial deregulation law considered but not enacted.
   (C) Law introduced but no Committee vote.
   (D) Law considered and defeated.
   (E) None was considered.
   (F) Regulation increased.

5. Common carrier authority -- support required for grant.

   (A) Requires proof of public convenience and necessity
   (B) Requires proof of public need and demand.
   (C) Requires proof of fitness only.
   (D) Less stringent proof required.
   (E) Automatic grant: similar to present ICC practice

6. Contract carrier authority -- support required for grant.

   (A) Requires proof of public need or interest
   (B) Requires only proof of a shipper's desire for service.
   (C) Automatic grant -- similar to present ICC practice.

7. Protest to Applications.

   (A) Denial, if existing service is proven to be satisfactory.
   (B) Carriers' protests will be considered and may result in denial.
   (C) Carriers may protest but protest is rarely successful.
   (D) Applications are rarely or never protested.

8. Hauling of certain commodities was made exempt from regulation within the past two years.

   (A) Many commodities were exempted from regulation
   (B) Limited number were exempted.
   (C) Exemptions similar to ICC's were adopted.
   (D) No change during period.

9. State regulation of rates.

   (A) Strict regulation.
   (B) Limited regulation.
   (C) Very little control exercised over rates.
   (D) No control exercised over rates.

10. Rate bureaus.

    (A) Exist and state law provides for antitrust immunity.
    (B) Exist, but no antitrust immunity provided under state law.
    (C) Terminated because of antitrust laws.
    (D) Terminated because of law enacted.
    (E) Terminated by act of regulatory Commission.

11. Sunsetting of regulatory Commission

    (A) Legislation was passed which sunsetted the Commission.
    (B) Legislation passed that may sunset regulatory Commission.
    (C) Sunset regulation was considered and defeated.
    (D) No sunset legislation was proposed.
    (E) Sunset law was sunsetted.

12. Shippers and deregulation.

    (A) Shippers strongly campaigned for deregulation.
    (B) Advocates of deregulation, generally limited to the large shippers with substantial volumes of traffic.
    (C) Shippers have shown very little interest in deregulation
    (D) Advocates, generally, are : State Governor ____ Legislators ____ ; Commissioners ____

63

# References

Alexander, Donald L., "Motor Carrier Deregulation and Highway Safety: An Empirical Analysis," *Southern Economic Journal*, July 1992, *59:1*, 28-38.

Allen, W. Bruce *et al.*, *The Impact of State Economic Regulation of Motor Carriage on Intrastate and Interstate Commerce*, U.S. Department of Transportation Report DOT-T-90-12, May 1990.

Barnekov, Christopher C. and Kleit, Andrew N., "The Efficiency Effects of Railroad Deregulation in the United States," *International Journal of Transport Economics*, 1990, *17*, 21-36.

Burton, Mark L., "Railroad Deregulation, Carrier Behavior, and Shipper Response: A Disaggregated Analysis," *Journal of Regulatory Economics*, 1993, *5*, 417-434.

California Public Service Commission, *California's Trucking Industry: A Review of Regulatory Polices and Objectives*, A Report Submitted to the California Public Utilities Commission by the Strategic Planning Division, February 1988.

Douglas, George W. and Miller, James C. III, *Economic Regulation of Domestic Air Transport: Theory and Policy*, Washington: The Brookings Institution, 1974.

Hausman, Jerry A., "Information Costs, Competition, and Collective Ratemaking in the Motor Carrier Industry," *The American University Law Review*, 1983, *32*, 377-392.

Joskow, Paul J. and Rose, Nancy L., "The Effects of Economic Regulation," in *Handbook of Industrial Organization, Volume 2*, Richard Schmalensee and Robert Willig (eds.), Amsterdam: North Holland, 1989.

Keeler, Theodore E., "Deregulation and Scale Economies in the U.S. Trucking Industry: An Econometric Extension of the Survivor Principle," *Journal of Law and Economics*, October 1989, *XXXII(2)*, 229-253.

Klevorick, Alvin K., "Directions and Trends in Industrial Organization: A Review Essay on the *Handbook of Industrial Organization*" in *Brookings Papers on Economic Activity*, Martin N. Baily and Clifford Winston (eds.), Washington: The Brookings Institution, 1991.

Lanning, Joyce A., Morrisey, Michael A., and Ohsfeldt, Robert L., "Endogenous Hospital Regulation and Its Effects on Hospital and Non-Hospital Expenditures," *Journal of Regulatory Economics*, 1991, *3*, 137-154.

Mathios, Alan D. and Rogers, Robert P., "The Impact of Alternative Forms of State Regulation on Direct Dial Intrastate Telephone Rates," *RAND Journal of Economics*, Autumn 1989, *20*, 437-453.

Motor Carrier Ratemaking Study Commission, *Collective Ratemaking in the Trucking Industry*, A Report to the President and the Congress, June 1983.

Tye, William B., *Encouraging Cooperation Among Competitors: The Case of Motor Carrier Deregulation and Collective Ratemaking*, New York: Quorum Books, 1987.

U.S. Department of Transportation, *New Entry into the Regulated Motor Carrier Industry*, Contract No. DOT-OS-80047, prepared by Sobotka & Co., Inc. and Mandex, Inc., December 19, 1979.

U.S. Department of Transportation, *Secretary's Task Force on Competition in the U.S. Domestic Airline Industry*, February 1990.

U.S. General Accounting Office, *Railroad Regulation: Economic and Financial Impacts of the Staggers Rail Act of 1980*, GAO/RCED-90-80, May 1990.

Wilson, Wesley W., and Dooley, Frank J., "An Empirical Model of Market Access," *Southern Economic Journal*, July 1993, *60*, 49-62.

Winston, Clifford, Corsi, Thomas M., Grimm, Curtis M., and Evans, Carol A., *The Economic Effects of Surface Freight Deregulation*, Washington: The Brookings Institution, 1990.

Ying, John S. and Keeler, Theordore E., "Pricing in a Deregulated Environment: The Motor Carrier Experience," *RAND Journal of Economics*, Summer 1991, *22*, 264-273.

www.ingramcontent.com/pod-product-compliance
Lightning Source LLC
Chambersburg PA
CBHW081254180526
45170CB00007B/2419